Tort Law in Uruguay

Tort Law in Uruguay

Mariana Barúa

This book was originally published as a monograph in the International Encyclopaedia of Laws/Tort Law.

Founding Editor: Roger Blanpain
General Editor: Frank Hendrickx
Volume Editor: Britt Weyts

Wolters Kluwer

Published by:
Kluwer Law International B.V.
PO Box 316
2400 AH Alphen aan den Rijn
The Netherlands
E-mail: lrs-sales@wolterskluwer.com
Website: www.wolterskluwer.com/en/solutions/kluwerlawinternational

Sold and distributed by:
Wolters Kluwer Legal & Regulatory U.S.
7201 McKinney Circle
Frederick, MD 21704
United States of America
E-mail: customer.service@wolterskluwer.com

ISBN 978-94-035-0076-8

e-Book: ISBN 978-94-035-4855-5
web-PDF: ISBN 978-94-035-4865-4

This title is available on www.kluwerlawonline.com

The Author

Mariana Barúa was born on 24 March 1979 in Lima, Perú. She graduated from the University of Lima/Peru, becoming a Juris Doctor, in 2004, *magna cum laude*. She also undertook part of her studies at the University of Santiago de Compostela, Spain. She practised law for five years in Lima and, afterwards, moved to Montevideo and has been practising law there ever since (for which she obtained the validation of her law degree in Uruguay, in 2010).

She received her LLM from the University of California, Davis, in 2008, and a Master's Degree in Civil Law (specializing in Contracts) at the Catholic University of Uruguay.

She was appointed as a Professor for Civil Law at the University of the Republic of Uruguay in 2016.

Mariana Barúa is the author of several articles and has also contributed to several books and journals.

The Author

Table of Contents

List of Abbreviations

ASSE	*Administración de los Servicios de Salud del Estado* – The State Health Administration
CC	*Código Civil* – Uruguayan Civil Code
CONARP	*Consejo Nacional de Autorregulación Publicitaria* – Self-regulation of Advertising National Council
CP	*Código Penal* – Uruguayan Criminal Code
HMO	Health Maintenance Organization
SCJ	*Suprema Corte de Justicia* – Supreme Court of Justice
SOA	*Seguro Obligatorio de Automotores* – Automobile Mandatory Insurance
SSR	*Superintendencia de Seguros y Reaseguros* (Insurance and Reinsurance Superintendence)
TAC	Civil Court of Appeal
UI	*Indexed Unit*
UNASEV	*Unidad Nacional de Seguridad Vial* – National Unit of Road Security
UR	*Adjustable Unit*

List of Abbreviations

General Introduction

§1. The General Background of the Country

I. Geography

1. Uruguay is a small country located in the southern region of South America, lying between Argentina and Brazil. Uruguay has a territorial area of approximately 176,000 square kilometres and is the second smallest country in South America, after Suriname. Uruguay is bound by Argentina, Brazil and the Atlantic Ocean. The capital of Uruguay is Montevideo, with a population of 1,377,617 (the last census was conducted in 2013).[1]

2. Uruguay has a population of 3,440,157. Of this, 48.34% are male and 51.66% are female. Further, 21.42% of the population are less than 15 years of age, 13.84% are more than 64 years old and 64.74% are aged between 15 and 64 years old.

3. Ethnic composition in Uruguay can be described by pointing out that most Uruguayan citizens have, mainly, Italian and Spanish ancestors. According to the last census, 94% of Uruguayans believe they have white ancestors, 8% believe they have Afro-American ancestors and 5% believe they have Indian ancestors. Of the population older than ten years, 2% do not know how to read and write (in the rural areas, this percentage is 3). A small 2% of the people living in Uruguay were born abroad. Of this percentage, most of them were born in Argentina, Brazil, Spain and Italy.

4. Life expectancy in Uruguay is 73.24 years for men and 80.20 years for women. Regarding employment, in July 2017, 7.76% of its population were unemployed.[2] According to the World Bank, Uruguay has the highest per capita income in South America.[3]

5. Since 1991, Uruguay has been a Member State of the MERCOSUR (*Mercado Común del Sur* – Southern Common Market), which is an ecopolitical agreement that currently has five sovereign members: Argentina, Brazil, Paraguay,

1. http://www.ine.gub.uy/documents/10181/39317/Uruguay_en_cifras_2014.pdf/aac28208-4670-4e96-b8c1-b2abb93b5b13.
2. http://www.ine.gub.uy/.
3. https://negocios.elpais.com.uy/noticias/uruguay-mayor-riqueza-per-capita-latinoamerica.html.

Uruguay (foundational members) and Venezuela (became a member in 2006 but, afterwards, was suspended in August 2017). Bolivia is in the process of becoming a member. Chile, Colombia, Ecuador, Guyana, Perú and Suriname currently have the status of 'associate member'.[4]

II. History

6. Before the Spanish colonization, Uruguay was the land of the Charrúas Tribe. The Spanish arrived in Uruguay in 1516. At the same time Spain started colonizing Uruguay's land, the Portuguese also advanced its colonization from Brazil towards Uruguayan territory. The first Spanish permanent colony was founded in 1624 at Soriano, meanwhile, the first colony of the Portuguese was founded in 1669 in Colonia del Sacramento.

7. Montevideo, Uruguay's capital, was founded by the Spanish in 1724, and its natural harbour soon developed into a commercial area competing with the Buenos Aires harbour. Spain and Portugal fought for the region throughout the seventeenth century. Spain ultimately prevailed and established the *Virreinato del Río de la Plata* (Platine River Virreinato).

8. In 1810, General José Gervasio Artigas led a revolution formed by people from present-day Uruguay and Buenos Aires, and, in 1814, Spanish authorities had to leave the country after being defeated by the revolution troops.

9. In 1815, a national government was formed. Nevertheless, in 1816, Brazilian forces invaded Uruguay and after four years of struggle, Brazilian forces conquered the Banda Oriental and named it *Provincia Cisplatina.*

10. On 25 August 1825, the Thirty-Three Orientals, led by Juan Antonio Lavalleja, with the support of the United Provinces of the Rio de la Plata (which today is Argentina) declared the independence of Uruguay. After this declaration, a war called the Cisplatine War took place. After 500 days of fighting, in 1828, both sides, with the intervention of the United Kingdom, agreed to sign the Treaty of Montevideo.

11. After the signing of this treaty, Uruguay became an independent country. Uruguay's first Constitution was adopted on 18 July 1830.

III. Political System

12. Uruguay, after its independence, organized itself, politically, as a Democratic Republic, a Unitary State formed by nineteen departments, with Montevideo as the capital city. The Uruguayan Constitution is the basis for all other statutes, and

4. http://www.mercosur.int/innovaportal/v/7823/11/innova.front/paises-del-mercosur.

its modification requires the affirmative vote of two-thirds of the total of the members of the House of Representatives (*Cámara de Diputados*) and of the Senate (*Cámara de Senadores*). It can also be modified with the approval of a national referendum.

13. The guiding principles of the Uruguayan Constitution are the following:

- the republican principle;
- the democratic principle;
- the principle of legality;
- the separation of powers principle (Legislative, Executive and Judicial Powers).

14. The republican principle is established in Articles 1, 2 and 3 of the Uruguayan Constitution and refers to a form of government in which monarchy is prohibited. While the democratic principle is established in Article 82 of the Uruguayan Constitution and states that the nation's sovereignty belongs to the citizens who, directly or through elected representatives, will practice it through the enactment of the laws that will govern them.

15. The principle of legality is established in Article 18 of the Uruguayan Constitution and states that the law will determine the order and formalities of the trials.

16. The principle of separation of powers is established in section IV of the Constitution in which the Executive Power, the Legislative Power and the Judicial Power are described.

17. The Executive Power has a structure in which the head is the President. The President is elected along with the Vice President for a five-year term. The President cannot be re-elected after the end of the five years term but can run for the presidency again for an alternate term after another President is elected and concludes his administrative term.

18. To win an election, a candidate has to obtain more than 50% of the citizen votes. In case an absolute majority is not obtained, the first and second most voted candidates will compete for the presidency.

19. The President appoints the Ministers, which are the head of the Ministries, in Uruguay, there are thirteen Ministries: National Defence, Social Development, Economy and Finance, Education and Culture, Farming, Cattle Raising and Fishing, Industry, Energy and Mining, Defence, Foreign Affairs, Public Health, Work and Social Security, Transportation and Public Constructions, Tourism and Sports, Housing, Land Use Planning and Environment.

20. The Legislative Power is administered by the Uruguayan General Assembly, which is formed by two chambers: the Chamber of Senators (*Senadores*), which is composed of thirty Senators, and the Chamber of Representatives (Diputados), which is formed by ninety-nine Representatives. Senators and Representatives are elected for a five-year term and can be re-elected.

21. Uruguay also has local governments, one in each of its nineteen departments. Each local government has a Governor (*Intendente*) who represents the Executive Power of the Department, and a Local Assembly (*Junta Departamental*), which is the Legislative Power of the Department.

22. In 2009, the *Alcaldías* were created in towns of more than 5,000 inhabitants. These *Alcaldías* are committees, with five members, where one of them is the President. Also, Montevideo has been divided into regions and *Alcaldías* have been created for each one of them.

IV. Economic and Social Values

23. Years after its independence (1825), in 1870, Uruguay became a supplier of livestock and crops. Uruguay experienced economic prosperity until 1913 when the depression began due to the international financial crisis. Also, during World War I, the export of basic commodities was blocked. Only in 1925, Uruguay recovered the livestock production levels it had before the crisis.

24. After the Great Depression, which originated in the United States in 1929, Uruguay changed its economic structure, protecting its industry and refraining from the import of foreign products.

25. From 1945 to 1955, the Uruguayan economy had its greatest growth, turning into one of the most important economies in South America. Because of this growth, the Uruguayan Government decided to acquire international companies and establish monopolies in order to provide access to services to the Uruguayan population. Among others, in 1948, Uruguay acquired the railroad which was owned by England.

26. Between 1960 and 1970, Uruguay exceedingly invested in its local industry, a decision that affected the Uruguayan economy negatively. This situation and the dispute regarding the distribution of the remaining State funds were some of the reasons leading to the military coup that took place in 1973, after which a dictatorship was established until 1985. Because of this, investments declined and savings were transferred abroad. This gave place to an economic crisis that lasted for several years. In 1974, the Uruguayan Government established the 'commercial dollar',[5] which had a value valid for foreign transactions (exports and imports), and the 'financial dollar', which was used for the rest of the economic operations.

27. In 1978, the government decided to unify the exchange rate. This was known as 'the *tablita cambiaria*' (the exchange board). This system sought to reduce the

5. http://historico.elpais.com.uy/especiales/aniversario/1980/1982/1.html.

inflation, using it as an anchor for the exchange rate. After this measure, the inflation outgrew the American dollar, causing an 'exchange rate backwardness'. This further caused Uruguay to enter into a severe indebtedness in American dollars, both of the country as well as of Uruguayan companies. This was known in the eighties as the 'Foreign Debt' crisis.

28. Between 1978 and 1982, the cheapening of the dollar and the opening of the economy encouraged the entry of imported products. This phenomenon occurred in the neighbour countries too, significantly increasing the number of tourists in the region. The imports caused a huge damage to the local industry. The government, as well as the industry, took several loans and started consuming this money.

29. In 1982, the Central Bank started losing international reserves, and in November of that year, the Minister of Economy and Finance announced that the exchange regime had to be abandoned and that the 'board' was broken. Inflation increased significantly and salaries lost 40% of their value. The country found itself with an external debt of USD 2,000 million, with the productive sectors badly affected and in debt and the financial institutions in serious trouble. The State had to save several institutions and the people lost their jobs. Uruguay and all of Latin America, where this economic model had been implemented, started the so-called lost decade. After 'the board' was broken, and after the end of the dictatorship, the country slowly returned to institutionalism.

30. During the 1990s, the economic model based on the import of products was substituted with one based on the export of products, mainly commodities and services to the region. Uruguay, in these decades, became known as a supplier of raw materials and food. It also became known for its expertise in tourism, intellectual property and financial services. After Uruguay took back protectionism from the industrial sector, several industries went bankrupt.

31. The economy progressed between 1990 and 1998. Nevertheless, in 2002, Uruguay suffered from a major economic crisis. This crisis began when the Argentineans travelled to Uruguay to withdraw their funds (Argentina had blocked its citizen's access to their banking accounts due to the crisis). In this period, as Alan Cage points out,[6] the American Dollar's value doubled (from 14 per one Uruguayan peso in January of 2002 to 31 in September of 2002). Also, the Uruguayan unemployment rate increased from 14% to 19%. Fifteen banks closed and several companies went bankrupt.

32. It is said that Uruguay learnt lessons from this crisis because, in 2008, Uruguay did not suffer the global crisis (which originated in the United States) and was one of the two economies in Latin America that grew in that period.

---

6. Alan Cage, 'El Ciclo Económico', Breve Historia Económica del Uruguay, p. 3.

33. Currently, Uruguay is considered an attractive place to invest. According to Uruguay XXI,[7] the reasons for this are the following:

- Political, legal, and social stability: Uruguay has a democratic system with institutional and legal stability, which guarantees a positive business environment and respect for the regulatory framework.
- Macroeconomic stability: In 2019, Uruguay reached the longest period of economic growth in its history, consolidating seventeen years of expansion at an average annual rate of 3.8%.
- Preferential market access: Uruguay is a member of Mercosur and has signed an FTA with Mexico. This makes it the gateway to a potential market with 550 million people.
- Investor benefits: Uruguay offers significant incentives for foreign and domestic investors, which are related to aspects such as taxes, and the Free-Trade Zone and Free Port and Airport systems.
- Ease of doing business: Uruguay guarantees equal treatment for investors and a restriction-free operation for business activity.
- Modern logistics: Uruguay's first-class port infrastructure, road network, and Free Port system make it the best logistics platform in the Mercosur region, as well as an advantageous distribution centre for goods in transit.
- Leader in ICT: Uruguay leads the ICT Development Index for Latin America (ITU, 2017). It is also the first and only country in South America to be part of D9, the group of the world's most advanced states in digital governance.
- Competitive national talent: Uruguay was the first country to implement the 'One Laptop per Child' programme. It has full digital inclusion, free education, everyday use of English and Portuguese, and a State-run university accessible to everyone.
- Efficient energy policies: Uruguay is one of the Latin American countries with the highest investment in clean energy and it is also at the forefront of the global production of electricity from wind power. During 2017–2020 period, 97% of electricity was produced from renewable sources, 32% of which came from wind farms.
- Excellent quality of living: Montevideo has the best quality of living in Latin America (Mercer, 2019). Also, Uruguay is the country with the highest and best-distributed income in the region.
- The country's significant growth over the past decade is related to a strong increase in investments: In Uruguay, Foreign Direct Investment (FDI) has reached record levels, which has allowed the country to become one of the main FDI destinations in South America over the past decade, in terms of GDP. Investors trust Uruguay due to the profitability obtained and the good business environment, in addition to being a country with an investment grade.
- Strategic location: Uruguay has a strategic location as a gateway to Mercosur, and two of its main ports, Montevideo and Nueva Palmira, are located at the end of

7. https://www.uruguayxxi.gub.uy/uploads/informacion/547d1df4f16265c270cf362f1a4b51779ad0706e.pdf

the Parana-Paraguay-Uruguay river system. Its time zone, between the US and Europe, makes the country a great complement to our global services to the region and the world.
- An excellent environment for business: Laws that protect and ensure equal treatment for both foreign and local investors, a free exchange market and a single tax system throughout the country are some of the conditions that make Uruguay an attractive and safe destination for business.
- Highly attractive tax benefits: Uruguay offers a wide array of incentives adapted to the different business sectors that can be developed in the country, e.g., industry, trade, or services: (i) Investment promotion system (Investment Law) – 20% to 100% refund of invested amounts; (ii) Free-trade zone – Users get 100% tax free; (iii) Temporary admission of raw materials and supplies; (iv) Only South American country with free airport regime, in addition to being the only one on the South American Atlantic coast with a free port regime.
- A country with an investment grade: Uruguay is a country with an investment grade ratified by the main credit rating agencies: Moody's, Standard & Poor's, Fitch Ratings, DBRS and R & I. Some of the reasons behind this vote of confidence for Uruguay were its macroeconomic balance and stability, an incremental diversification of the economy, and its efficient debt-management strategy.

34. Also, in Uruguay, clear rules can be found, taking into account that:

- According to the economic freedom rankings (2021), made by Heritage Foundation, Uruguay is ranked second in South America and is ranked forty-fourth in the overall ranking.
- According to the political stability rankings (2020), developed by World Bank's Worldwide Governance Indicators, Uruguay is ranked sixteenth and first in terms of political stability in Latin America.[8]
- According to the corruption perception index (2020), prepared by Transparency International, Uruguay is ranked twenty-first out of 180 countries and is the first country in Latin America in terms of reliability and low levels of corruption.
- Finally, the global competitiveness index (20172018), made by the World Economic Forum, places Uruguay as the fifth most competitive country for business in Latin America, after Chile, Mexico, Colombia and Peru and is ranked seventy-sixth in the overall ranking.[9]

35. Finally, we deem it important to point out that the magazine *The Economist*, chose Uruguay as its 2013 'Country of the Year'.

---

8. http://www.theglobaleconomy.com/rankings/wb_political_stability/.
9. https://reports.weforum.org/global-competitiveness-index-2017-2018/competitiveness-rankings/

§2. Legal System

I. Primacy of Legislation and Codification

36. In Uruguay, the principle of separation of powers is applied. The country is politically organized as a republic with a democratic government system that has three independent powers.

37. As was already said, the principle of separation of powers is established in section IV of the Constitution in which the Executive Power, the Legislative Power and the Judicial Power are described. The Uruguayan legal system consists of statutory law, which is passed by the Congress and, afterwards, ratified by the President.

38. The most important source of law in Uruguay is the Constitution. Second in the hierarchy, the laws are applied, and in third place, the decrees. Therefore, if a decree goes against a law, the law will prevail, and the same applies to the law and the Constitution. This is known as the Kelsen Pyramid, in which the Constitution goes first. And lastly, we can find the regulations. Uruguay is a Civil law country; therefore, decisions issued by judges in individual cases are not binding for other judges in future cases. Court rulings might guide judges but they are not a primary source of law, as happens in the common law. Judges and administrative officers must consult statutory law and have to comply with it. They also have to interpret the law in accordance with specific rules.

39. Sometimes, the interpretation of a law can decide the outcome of a case. This is why the Civil Code of Uruguay establishes two rules regarding the interpretation of the law. Article 16 of the CC states that when a case cannot be solved by words or by the spirit of the law for the issue at hand, the judge must focus on the grounds of similar laws. If the latter does not help, he must refer to the general principles of law and the articles, books and magazines written by the most approved legal authors. Also, Article 17 of the CC states that: when the literal meaning of the law is clear, one cannot ignore it and attend to the spirit of the law. But if there is an obscure expression in the law, one can attend to its spirit, clearly expressed in the law, or to the history of its approval.

II. Position of the Judiciary

40. The Judicial Power is exercised by the Supreme Court of Justice (*Suprema Corte de Justicia*) and by the Courts of Appeals (*Tribunales*) and District Courts (*Juzgados* – JLC), in the way established by law.

41. The Supreme Court is the highest court of our country and is composed of five members. To be a member of the Supreme Court, a person has to be: (i) 40 years old, (ii) a Uruguayan natural citizen (exercising its citizenship) or a Uruguayan legal citizen who has exercised his citizenship for ten years and has lived in Uruguay for twenty-five years, (iii) a lawyer for at least ten years or a judge or public prosecutor for at least eight years.

42. Members of the Supreme Court are appointed by the General Assembly (Legislative Power) by two-thirds of its members. The General Assembly has to appoint the members of the Supreme Court in the following ninety days after the vacancy occurred. If this period passes and no appointment is made, the member of the Court of Appeal with higher seniority will automatically fill this vacancy. If there are two judges equal in seniority, the one with more years of experience in their judicial career or as a public prosecutor will take the vacancy.

43. The members of the Supreme Court are appointed for ten years in their positions and cannot be re-elected for a consecutive five-year period.

44. The Supreme Court has the following functions:

(1) It issues the final ruling in cases in which the judges of the Appellate Court revoke, unanimously, the ruling of the District Court, and one of the parties files an appeal for cassation against this second judgment. The matter discussed in the legal proceeding must amount to more than UR 4,000 (currently, USD 144,363), and the appeal can only be based on an error or infraction in the application of the law:
   (a) Rules in cases regarding:
      – Constitution offenders.
      – Treaties, pacts and conventions with other States.
      – Diplomats accredited in Uruguay.
      – Other cases, established by International Law.
   (b) Supervises the Appellate Courts, District Courts and the other offices of the Judicial Power in administrative matters (not regarding jurisdictional decisions).
   (c) Drafts the bill regarding the budget of the Judicial Power and submits it to the Executive Power so that it can be added to the other proposed budgets.
   (d) With the approval of the Senate, or when it is in recess, with the approval of the Permanent Commission, appoints the citizens that will be part of the Appellate Courts.
   (e) Appoints the judges.
   (f) Appoints the public defenders and judges of Peace.
   (g) Appoints, promotes and removes employees of the Judicial Power.
   (h) Solves the conflict of competence between the authorities of the Judicial Power and those of the Administrative Contentious Courts.
   (i) Bestows the position of judges.
   (j) Receives the oath from lawyers, public notaries and solicitors.
   (k) Oversees the correct practice of the professions mentioned above.
   (l) Passes decrees regarding the functioning of the Judicial Power.

45. Also, it is important to point out that the salaries of the members of the Supreme Court are determined by the Executive Power.

III. Distinction Between Public and Private Law

46. There are several positions regarding this matter. Some authors understand that when society or the State (and not as a private person) intervenes in the legal relation, we are in the public law sphere; meanwhile, when the relationship develops exclusively between individuals, we are in the private law sphere.

47. Other authors sustain that when the legal bond is established in a subordinated manner, we are before a public law relation. However, when the legal bond is created between individuals who are equals, legally speaking, we are before a private law relation. In the first case, the individual is forced to act in a certain way (i.e., pay taxes), while in the second, the individual decides to act in a certain way voluntarily (i.e., promise to pay a certain amount of money).

48. This theory is criticized because, according to some authors, there are public law relations in which the parties are equal (as occurs in international relations between States), and there are private law relations in which one individual is legally subordinated to the other (as is a contract between an employer and his employee).

49. Other authors maintain that the differences between public and private law are the interest at stake. Therefore, if the protected interest is a general interest, we are before a public law relation, while if the interest at stake is the interest of individuals, exclusively, we are before a private law relation.

50. This position is also criticized, arguing that there are some laws which protect a public interest and, at the same time, satisfy private interests (criminal law, for example). According to the Uruguayan Professor, Enrique Vescovi, all of the attempts to differentiate between public and private law are arguable because they contemplate some aspects of law but disregard the rest of them. Nevertheless, this professor understands that this attempt to distinguish them is useful and helps study the different branches of law.[10]

51. Public law is divided into several branches: Public International Law, Constitutional Law, Administrative Law and Criminal Law. Private law, which used to be identified with Civil law, also can be divided into several branches. When private law started to be divided into these branches, the equivalence between Civil law and Private law came to an end. The first separation of Private law was into Civil law and Procedural law (which is a branch of law shared by private and public law). Afterwards, the evolution of commerce and commercial activities generated the necessity for the creation of a new branch of law: Commercial Law.

10. *See* E. Vescovi, Introducción al Derecho (17th ed., 1992), pp. 31–32.

Afterwards, the complexity of the relations between individuals from different nationalities generated the necessity for the creation of a new branch of law: Private International Law.

52. Also, there are other branches of law, that were created recently, which present the characteristic of having been taken from both public and private law at the same time, and also from the Economic and Financial Science: Financial Law, Labour Law, Agrarian Law, Aeronautical Law, etc.

IV. Sources of Private Law in General and of Tort Law in Particular

A. *Sources of Law in the Uruguayan Legal System*

53. Before analysing the sources of private law, in general, and of tort law, in particular, we deem it important to mention the sources of law of the Uruguayan legal system. There are several notions of the sources of law. For example, they are referred to as sources of knowledge, referring to what is and has been historically – 'law', trying to understand it through the study of ancient documents, legislative collections, etc.

54. Some have also referred to sources of inspirations, relating to the sources in which the legislator inspires to write a specific law. Some authors have referred to the sources as the creative force of law, asking themselves if it emerges from human nature, the legal ideals, the social life, the economy, etc.

55. Nevertheless, the sources which are legally binding are the formal sources. Formal sources are, according to Boneccasse, the mandatory and predetermined ways that laws must abide in order to be able to impose coercively.[11]

56. Therefore, it is not important to know the origin of a law or the source of inspiration for the creation of it, but the way it has manifested, to know if it is binding or not.

57. In Uruguay, the only formal source of law is the law. The other sources of law are material sources and, therefore, are only binding when the law determines so.

58. There are four sources of the Uruguayan legal system (applicable to all branches, including private law): legislation (laws), custom, case law and the settled/official view among commentators or academics.

11. *Ibid.*, p. 71.

1. Legislation (Law)

59. The law can be expressed in different ways: through law, costume, etc. Legislation is the group of legal rules issued by a competent authority of the State.[12] Under the term 'legislation', we understand it to be comprised of the law issued by the Legislative Power, as well as the decree of the Departmental Council, or the decree passed by the Mayor or Executive Power.

60. In Uruguayan positive law, legislation is the only formal source of law. When a legal rule takes the form of legislation, meaning that it is passed by a competent authority, it is mandatory.

2. Custom

61. The customary law is the law that is formed unconsciously among a society, after the repetition of the same practice time and again, and due to the conviction of this society that this practice is necessary and mandatory.[13] Custom is, therefore, formed by two elements: a material element – the repetition of an act – and other psychological – the certainty that this act is binding and that from its violation will result in punishment.

62. This practice must be general, and constant, and perceived as mandatory. Some authors have sustained that for a custom to legally exist, it must be applied in case law. Therefore, if several judicial rulings apply the custom, then it becomes a legal custom. This opinion has been disregarded by other authors who argue that when a judge issues a ruling, he applies the rule of law: he does not create the rule, he only applies it. Therefore, for the case law to apply a custom, it first has to exist legally.

63. Custom is very important for Uruguayan law because it nurtures law with social reality. Social reality varies depending on the historical moment and place, and, therefore, in a way, custom updates the law. Nevertheless, as was already said, custom is not a formal source of law in the Uruguayan legal system.

64. Article 9 of the Civil Code states: 'Laws cannot be abrogated by other than other laws; and it will not be possible to allege against its abidance the lack of use or the custom or practice against it. Custom does not constitute law, unless in cases in which law refers to it (Article 594, numeral 2).' And numeral 2 of Article 594 of the CC, regarding the dividing wall between two buildings, states: 'The height of the dividing line will be determined by the regulations that may exist, and by the custom which should be constant and well-known.'

---

12. *Ibid.*, pp. 72–73.
13. *Ibid.*, pp. 73–78.

65. Article 1834 of the CC states: 'He who provided some work or render some service to another can claim the price even though no price or payment was agreed, as long as the service or work referred to his profession or honest way of life. In this case, it will be presumed that the interested parties agreed to a custom price, to be determined judicially, if there was doubt.' This is an example of a law giving the force of law to a custom. In this case, as can be noted, the law (formal source) to be applied will need the content provided by the custom (material source).

66. As a conclusion of this chapter, it can be established that in our positive law, following the trend of the French Revolution, the law has an absolute predominance and even in cases of legal loopholes, judges are not authorized to recur to custom (which is an option that has been adopted by the most modern Codes, such as the Chinese Code, the Swiss Code, etc.).

3. Case Law

67. Case law has been defined as the way in which laws are interpreted by courts or as a group of judicial rulings established regarding a specific issue.[14] When there is a loophole or doubt regarding the interpretation of a law, judges, when applying it, must give their position and when the thesis is reiterated (in several rulings), it is said that there is case law.

68. Strictly speaking, it would be enough with only one ruling to be able to state that there is case law regarding an issue (which after some repeated rulings regarding this point, would become a 'leading case'). The role of the judge is to apply the law to the specific case.

69. For a long time, it was understood that – under the influence of the ideas of the French Revolution – the judge was simply an applier of rules, who had to abide by the law, and that rulings did not add anything new to the judicial order. Afterwards, the Vienna School, led by Kelsen, sustained that the judge, as well as the legislator, created rules, in these cases individualized, because due to the indeterminacy of laws, the judge, when applying the general rule, had a great leeway and its activity was an act of creation.

70. According to Professor Vescovi, although the judicial ruling is not an individualized rule and even though the judge applies the already existing rule, nevertheless, its function is one that of a lawmaker. The law cannot foresee everything and the judge cannot excuse from the ruling, alleging obscurity or insufficiency of the law, and because of this, his role in the creation of law is very important.

71. Without prejudice of this, in Uruguayan law, jurisprudence is not a formal source of law. The ruling of a judge in a certain case does not compel other judges,

14. *Ibid.*, pp. 78–82.

even when the other judge has a lower position. This opinion does not force judges at all. Even the same judge can rule differently in a future case regarding the same issue at hand.

72. The rule states that in our country, case law is not a formal source of law is Article 12 of the CC, which states: 'Only the legislator can explain or interpret law in a generally mandatory way. Judicial rulings are not binding in other cases different to the case in which they were issued.'

73. And Article 14 establishes: The High Court of Justice, anytime it deems it convenient, will inform the Legislative Power of the doubts and difficulties that occur in the intelligence and application of the law and about the loopholes perceived in them, in order to encourage, either the interpretation of the existing laws, or the passing of new laws. This is a very important power that should be used more often by our highest courts.

74. The disadvantage of not having case law as a formal source of law is that there is always a risk that in an exact case, two judges might rule differently. Therefore, in Uruguayan law, the outcome of a trial depends on the opinion of the judge knowing the specific case, who is appointed by the Office for the Reception and Distribution of Matters (ORDA). This fact generates uncertainty regarding the outcome of cases.

75. Nevertheless, the advantage of this system is that it allows the judge to have more leeway before the case at hand, permitting him to comply with the real purpose of case law, which is to apply justice to the specific case (materializing in this way the equity principle).

76. Another important thing to point out is that in Uruguay (as well as in other Civil law countries), despite the leeway judges have to rule as they deem fair, they are more and more influenced by case law. This is generating a trend of editorials increasingly publishing case law. Also, due to this trend, the Judicial Power has created an online register of all the rulings of the Appellate Court and the Supreme Court so that judges and lawyers can find out the trends of case law regarding a specific issue. Finally, it is important to note that case law is an important material source of law because it inspires the law and legislators should take inspiration from it in order to perfect the law.

4. Settled/Official View among Commentators or Academics

77. Even though the opinion of academics is not a formal source of law, Uruguayan law states that in case of loopholes, judges must refer to the most well-received opinions of academics (which turns it into a material source of law). Indeed, Article 16 of the CC states that:

> When a civil act occurs, and it cannot be solved by the words or by the spirit of law in the matter at hand, the grounds of analogue laws should be considered, and if even then the doubt subsist, then general principles of law and the opinion of academics should be considered, taking into account the case circumstances.

78. Legislators, as well as judges, are always aware of the opinion of the most important academics of Uruguay and abroad and frequently use these opinions as an inspiration for new laws or in order to justify their rulings. It is important to note, regarding this point, that the most well-received opinions of academics in Uruguay, in Civil law, are the ones of Professor Jorge Gamarra, Judge Beatriz Venturini, former Judge Dora Szafir, Professor Carlos de Cores Helguera, Professor Jaime Berdaguer, Professor Santiago Carnelli, Professor Gerardo Caffera Morandi, Professor Jorge Peirano Facio, among others. Finally, the last source of law is the General Principles of Law. As was already said in point 43, Article 16 of the UCC states that these principles can be applied when a civil act occurs and it cannot be solved by the words or the spirit of law. The Supreme Court of Justice (SCJ), in its ruling 246/2002 dated 9/9/2002, has stated, citing other authors, that these principles are 'Guidelines that inform to a law and inspire directly or indirectly a series of solutions for which they can be used to promote or guide the approval of new rules, advise on the interpretation of the ones in force, and resolve the cases not foreseen by laws' '(Plá Rodríguez, "Los principios del Derecho del trabajo", 2a. Ed., page. 9),' and that 'To solve an unforeseen matter in accordance with the general principles means, therefore, to rule as the lawmaker would have, in case he could have had knowledge of this specific case (García Maynez, "Introducción al estudio del derecho", page 372).'[15]

B. Sources of Private Law in General

79. As was already said, in Uruguay, the law can be divided into public and private law. Private law, as well, is divided into different branches of law: Civil Law, Commercial Law, International Law, etc. Civil law can be further divided into patrimonial and extra-patrimonial law. Extra-patrimonial law studies the individuals and their personality as well as family relations.

80. Patrimonial law (which is called in common law as 'private law') refers to the law of contracts and torts (as it is called in the common law) or the law of obligations, contracts and civil liability (as it is called in civil legal systems). Therefore, sources of Private Law (or civil patrimonial law) are studied in Uruguay as the sources of obligations.

81. Obligations, as will be seen afterwards, can refer to a civil wrong that causes someone else to suffer loss or harm resulting in the legal liability of the tortfeasor

15. *Vazquez, Jose y otros v. CUTCSA,* SCJ No. 246/2002 (2002).

or as a legal duty that arises from a mutual agreement or from law. In this case, the breach of this duty will give place to the legal liability of the offender.

82. Sources of obligations are five: the contract, the crime, the quasi-contract, the quasi-crime and the law. Historically, the contract is the oldest source of obligation. Although crime existed before the creation of the contract, the contract was identified as a source of obligations first. The quasi-contract is another source of obligations. In this case, there is an unlawful act that generates an obligation but in which the meeting of minds is lacking.

83. Another source of obligations is the quasi-crime, in which the offender does not have the will to commit the crime. Finally, the fifth source of the obligation is the law. This is because, besides obligations, or civil wrongs that arise from the above-mentioned sources, the law refers to other obligations that appear from special circumstances and that, when breached, generate civil wrongs.

84. Therefore, regarding the sources of obligations in Uruguayan law, we can find acts or sources that are normally intentional: the contract and the crime. There are two sources which are non-intentional: the quasi-contract and the quasi-crime. There are two sources which are legal (the contract and the quasi-contract) and two illegal ones (the crime and the quasi-crime). And in the middle, giving symmetry to all of this appears the law.[16]

85. Article 1246 of the CC states that:

> Obligations rise, from mutual assent of two or more individuals, as in the contracts, from a voluntary act of the individual obliged, as in the quasi-contracts; due to an act that has given place to harm or damage to another person, as in the crimes and quasi-crimes, or when the law states it, as in the family relations, or in the civil relations. Obligations that rise from the law are expressed in it.

C. Sources of Tort Law in Particular

86. Civil liability, which resembles tort law in Civil law countries, has three sources; they are circumstances or acts that, because of their nature, generate non-contractual liability.[17] Our law, following what was done in other legal systems, has regulated civil responsibility sources according to the particular acts that configure this responsibility. This way, the sources of civil responsibility are: liability for one's own acts, liability for the acts of others and liability for things (which includes liability for animals).

87. These types of liability will be analysed in Chapters I and II.

---

16. *See* J. Peirano Facio, Curso de Obligaciones, Tomo I, (1957), pp. 33–38.
17. *See* J. Peirano Facio, Responsabilidad Extracontractual (1954), p. 483.

§3. Function of the Law of Torts

88. Responsibility refers to the existence of a duty of the tortfeasor due to the damage caused to the victim. This duty can pursue two different types of purpose: restitution or punishment. Restitution supposes the feasibility of re-establishment to the situation existent before the wrongful act. Punishment is imposed in order to repair the fault of the tortfeasor, while compensation seeks to repair the damage suffered by the victim.[18]

89. While the compensation is a sanction that seeks to satisfy, the punishment seeks to punish the tortfeasor. The compensation is paid to repair the harm, while punishment is given just because the wrongful act was committed.

90. Our jurisprudence has pointed out that the objective and finality of the compensation is to comply not only with a reparatory purpose but also to punish the tortfeasor. Nevertheless, most judges understand that the compensation has to cover only the harm caused, dismissing, this way, the possibility of understanding this payment as a punishment.

§4. Relationship Between Torts and Criminal Law

91. Authors have differentiated both types of responsibilities, taking into account, among others, the following issues: (i) legal capacity (for criminal law, legal capacity begins at 18 years of age while in torts, legal capacity starts at 10); (ii) nature of sanctions (civil sanctions seek to repair the harm done, criminal sanctions aim to punish the behaviour of the delinquent); and (iii) competent jurisdiction (civil faults are judged by civil courts, while criminal faults are judged by criminal courts).[19]

92. An unlawful act can be a civil crime or a civil quasi-crime (and, therefore, the tortfeasor must compensate the victim) or a criminal crime or offence (if this is the case, the tortfeasor must be punished for this behaviour) or it can oblige, jointly, to payment of a reparation and punishment (convicted to serve jail time, for example) at the same time.

93. There is no technical explanation to explain the reason why an unlawful act is a civil fault and not a criminal one, or vice versa, or is both at the same time. The reason for this is political.

94. If an act is performed under the circumstances established by Article 1319 of the CC or by-laws which state, in specific cases, particular regimes of liability, and what the legislator seeks is to repair the harm done, then we are at civil fault

18. *Ibid.*, pp. 46–47.
19. *Ibid.*, pp. 26–30.

cases. On the other hand, criminal faults are regulated for multiple reasons: some of them have a traditional or historical background, others are incompatible with social order, etc.

95. Uruguayan jurisprudence has always established civil faults and criminal faults as independent of one another, to the extent that a person can commit a fault (i.e., regulated as a civil fault, as well as a criminal one) and be found innocent in criminal court while being condemned to pay a reparation in a civil court for the same fault.

§5. Relationship Between Contractual and Delictual or Tortious Responsibility

I. Relationship Between Contractual and Delictual Responsibility

96. In Uruguay, there is contractual responsibility when there is a breach regarding contractual duties agreed by parties and, also, every time a contractual duty, in general (notwithstanding which is its source), is breached. Even when the obligation is a legal or a quasi-contractual one, this applies. Meanwhile, if the breach does not refer to a contractual duty, then we will be talking about extra-contractual responsibility.

97. In contractual responsibility cases, the parties involved were linked before the breach by a contract (stated by law or convention). While in the extra-contractual liability cases, parties were not legally connected until the breach occurred.

98. Regarding extra-contractual liability, Uruguayan experts state that this is the result of the breach of the offender, of his general duty not to harm others (*neminem laedere*). It is a general duty due to the fact that it does not refer to a specific person but to all individuals in general. According to other authors, in extra-contractual liability, the duty breached is the one referred to as act with diligence, also called protection duty.[20]

99. Authors such as De Cupis state that we are at a case of contractual liability when a credit right is harmed, and we are at extra-contractual liability cases when an absolute subjective right is harmed.[21]

100. In regard to the question referred to the relationship between contractual and delictual responsibility, Gamarra understands that they are not the same, nor are

20. *See* Jorge Gamarra, 'Tratado de Derecho Civil Uruguayo', Tomo XX, Editorial FCU, Montevideo, 2003, pp. 25–26.
21. De Cupis, Danno, I, n. 13, pp. 67–68, cited by Gamarra, 'Tratado de Derecho Civil Uruguayo', Tomo XX, *supra*, p. 27.

they separated. There is a unity and also a dualism of civil responsibility in Uruguay. Civil responsibility is only one, and this can be appreciated when analysing the functional identity that exists in both types of responsibility: both share the same purpose to displace the damage burden from one party to another. They, too, perform the same function.

101. Contractual and delictual responsibility also share the traditional concept of responsibility, which consists in holding a person liable after a display of harmful behaviour which caused damage.[22]

II. Rule of Non-*cumul*

102. The *cumul* rule is applied when, to the same situation, both contractual (Article 1341) and extra-contractual regulations (Article 1319) can be applied. An example of this is the case of a transportation accident, in which the passenger celebrated a contract with the transportation company which was breached when the accident occurred (the passenger did not get to his destination on time), but, also, the passenger suffered physical damages (which constitute the breach of the general duty not to harm others – *neminem laedere*). The accident was only one, but the legal duties breached were two: one contractual and one extra-contractual.

103. In Uruguay, there is no regulation on the matter and, traditionally, courts have understood that the non-*cumul* rule was applicable and, therefore, every time a contract existed between the parties, the extra-contractual liability regulations would not apply.[23]

104. In his Civil Treaty, Professor Gamarra distinguishes between the *cumul* rule and the concurrence of liabilities. In the first one, the victim of wrongdoing can use, jointly or consecutively, the regulation of both liabilities in the same proceeding or in consecutive proceedings, while in the second one, the victim must choose the application of only one of those regulations.[24]

105. Uruguayan law does allow the *cumul* rule when the victim of the wrongdoing asks for compensation for contractual liability, and third parties ask for compensation for tortuous liability.

106. This usually happens, for example, in the claims filed in Uruguayan courts regarding alleged medical malpractice. In these cases, the patient asks for compensation for the breach of contract and their relatives, for the damage caused to them, for example, referred to pain and suffering, economic losses, etc.

---

22. *Ibid.*, p. 27.
23. *Ibid.*, p. 52.
24. *Ibid.*

107. It is also important to point out that Professor Blengio, in 1998, questioned the prohibition to apply the non-*cumul* rule.[25]

108. He stated that, after a malpractice, patients filed claims against medical institutions in which they sued the institution for contractual liability and the practising doctors for tortuous liability. Now, taking into account that the medical institution will have to answer if the doctor is found guilty (the principal must answer for its dependents acts), the victim of a medical malpractice can choose to sue the medical institution for contractual or extra-contractual liability. This way of filing a claim, nowadays, is accepted by courts.

109. Gamarra, in his treaty, establishes that, in his opinion, the *cumul* rule is applicable in Uruguay, with some exceptions, which are: (i) if the parties in the contract stated a limited liability clause, then one of the parties cannot try to avoid its application by suing for extra-contractual liability; (ii) if the parties agreed to reduce the statute of limitations, then this agreement cannot be voided by filing a lawsuit for extra-contractual liability.[26]

110. He explains his position, arguing that this option is the one that protects the victim the most (and, therefore, coincides with the Civil law principle that seeks the utmost protection for the victim – *favour victimae*). Also, he says that the ac*cumulation* of the regulation of both liabilities allows the victim to surpass some problems that arise from the separation of these regimes: the liability for acts of things can only be claimed by indirect victims of the wrongdoing and not by the patient, the duty of security will benefit the patient but not his relatives, the statute of limitations for a breach of contract is of ten years, and for extra-contractual liability, it is of four years.[27]

III. Pre-contractual Liability

111. Regarding pre-contractual liability, it is not regulated in Uruguay, where only two responsibilities are consecrated: the contractual and the extra-contractual liability. Therefore, the pre-contractual liability must be considered under one of them. Some authors understand that the pre-contractual liability, such as the extra-contractual liability, refers to a duty to refrain from causing harm to others (*neminem laedere*) and to a generic duty to act with good faith. Also, they point out that, until a contract is signed, all that happens before will refer to extra-contractual liability.

112. However, some authors understand that, due to the fact that some of the Articles of the CC (1672, 1717, 1721, 1804, 2059, 2075, 2078, 2204, 2205, 2236,

25. Blengio, Juan, 'La Cuestión del concurso y del cúmulo de la responsabilidad civil. Reseña sobre un tema que es conveniente volver a reflexionar', ADCU XXVII, Editorial FCU, p. 453.
26. Gamarra, 'Tratado de Derecho Civil Uruguayo', Tomo XX, *supra*, p. 61.
27. *Ibid.*, p. 68.

2249), as well as some laws, refer to this type of liability (Article 4, letter i, and Article 27 of Law 8.733) and, when doing so, if they refer to particular duties, specific actions directed to a determinate person, then we definitely are in the field of contractual liability when referring to the pre-contractual stage.

113. One other argument that these authors argue, is that the pre-contractual stage occurs due to a voluntary act of the parties negotiating, while the extra-contractual field refers to cases in which the parties usually get in contact after the damage is caused.[28]

§6. Protected Interests

114. In Uruguay, not all damages are compensated. For the damage to be subject to compensation, it has to receive, previously, a legal qualification (formal element of the harm, which adds to the physical element). A situation in law is irrelevant unless a law qualifies it. Indeed, law, through the qualification of a situation, which implies the assessment of an interest, considered in itself and in relation to the interest of the community, issues a positive judgment regarding its protection.[29]

115. Not all situations are considered relevant in order to be qualified by law. Indeed, immoral interests are not protected because they receive a negative qualification. For example, in Uruguay, a prostitute cannot file a complaint for breach of contract.

116. However, there are other interests that, even though they do not receive a negative qualification, are not protected anyway because no law endorses them. This was the case of the right of a domestic partner to claim compensation after separating from his partner until some years ago, when jurisprudence understood this person to have a right to claim compensation (and afterwards, Act 18.246, enacted on 10 January 2018, established, in some circumstances, similar rights for domestic partners to the ones of spouses).

117. Forces of nature can cause damages (earthquakes, for example), but these damages cannot be compensated. This is due to the fact that compensable damages are only those caused by men, directly or indirectly (this is established in Article 1319, which, in the beginning, states that 'Any unlawful act performed by a man, that causes harm to another, ...'

118. Another damage that cannot be compensated is self-injury. This is because Article 1319 states that the harm has to be caused by 'another' person.

---

28. *Ibid.*, pp. 149–150.
29. Pugliatti, Esecuzione forzata e diritto sostanziale, pag. 62, Milano, 1933, cited by Jorge Gamarra, 'Tratado de Derecho Civil Uruguayo', Tomo XIX, 2 Edition, Editorial Fundación de Cultura Universitaria, Montevideo, 2012, p. 284.

119. Damages will not be compensated if there is a cause of justification; as for example, when exercising a right. Indeed, Article 1321 points out that he who exercises his right does not harm others, which means that even though the exercise of a right may harm others, this harm will not be subject to compensation.

120. The requirement for damages to be compensated is that these damages are caused unlawfully. Lawful damages will not be compensated. Nevertheless, there can be some damages which, notwithstanding its lawful cause, must be compensated anyways; for example, in the case of the traffic accidents, mandatory insurance in which, even though the insurance holder did not cause the accident, the insurance must compensate the victim anyways (Article 6 of Act 18.412).[30]

121. Regarding the persons that can ask for the compensation for the harm caused, in Uruguay, the most accepted doctrine understands that these people can be divided into the following groups: first, the victim, and then, the people most closely related to the victim: his father, son, husband, etc. In these cases, as well as in the case in which the victim asks for compensation, the harm when proven has to be compensated by the tortfeasor. It is understood that these persons have the right to be compensated because they have a right to alimony.

122. Finally, other people that can ask for compensation are people related to the victim, such as the girlfriend, the partner, sponsor, etc. In these cases, the claimants do not have a right of alimony regarding the victim, but, nevertheless, the victim might as well pay their expenses. And therefore, the death or serious harm to the victim generates an economic setback for these persons.

123. In this regard, Peirano Facio understands that any claimant who proves that the harm of the victim has caused him harm as well can ask legitimately for compensation. While Gamarra has sustained that the plaintiff has to have a subjective right, or at least a legal interest or a legal situation that gives him the right to ask for compensation.[31]

30. Gamarra, 'Tratado de Derecho Civil Uruguayo', Tomo XIX, *supra*, pp. 235–236.
31. *Ibid.*, pp. 277–284.

Part I. Liability for One's Own Acts

Chapter 1. General Principles

124. The authors understand that this type of liability refers to the general regime of responsibility regulated by Article 1319 of the CC. This article establishes the following:

> Every unlawful act of men that causes harm to another imposes to the individual whose willful misconduct, fault or negligence has generated the harm, the duty to repair it.
>
> When the unlawful act has been performed with willful misconduct, that is, with intent to harm, it constitutes a crime, when the will to harm is missing; the unlawful act constitutes a quasi-crime. In one case and in the other, the unlawful act can be negative or positive, depending this on the duty infringed, and if it referred to a duty to do, or to refrain from doing.

§1. Unlawfulness and Fault

125. If an objective type of unlawfulness is accepted (infringement of a right, interest or a legally protected situation), then there is no difficulty differentiating unlawfulness from fault (to act without the diligence of a good father of the family). On the contrary, if a subjective notion of unlawfulness is applied (behaviour of the offender that breaches a duty), then the confusion is so important that it has even been said that there cannot be unlawfulness without fault.[32]

126. The first difficulty refers to the fact that if all persons have the duty to act as good fathers of families, in order to not cause harm to the others (a rule that can be extracted from Article 1319 of the CC), then any violation of this duty should result in an act that would be, at the same time, unlawful and at fault.

127. This is why all the behaviours at fault (to ignore a stop sign or to drive without wearing seat belts) would be also unlawful and would, therefore, make it impossible to differentiate fault from unlawfulness. This distinction is not strictly necessary, at least in other legal systems like the French one, in which the law

32. Jorge Luis Gamarra, and Jorge Gamarra, 'Responsabilidad Extracontractual', Editorial Fundación de Cultura Universitaria, 1st ed., Montevideo, 2007, pp. 19–22.

(Article 1382 of the French CC[33]) does not require unlawfulness as a requisite separated and independent from fault. Nevertheless, in our legislation, Article 1319 of the CC states unlawfulness as an autonomous requirement, separated and independent from fault, and because of this, the said separation must be made.

128. As regards this point, it is interesting to mention a case in which a person stumbles over a jack and falls to the floor, suffering injuries. In this case, the District Court ruled in favour of the defendant, stating that it was not proven the unlawful act and, therefore, the fault. This ruling proves the confusion that exists regarding unlawfulness and fault.

129. This ruling was appealed, and the Appellate Court ruled in favour of the plaintiff, saying that:

> the unlawfulness was verified in this case by the injuries suffered by Mrs. N.A. after bumping into the object left in the sidewalk, and establishes that even in the subjective thesis the ruling would be the same, because this act would have violated Article 53 of the General Ordinance of Traffic (Article 590 of the Digest).[34]

130. Therefore, this difference can be summed up by stating that an act can be at fault without the need for it to cause harm (e.g., when breaching a law, such as the transit ordinance), while an act will only be unlawful when it causes harm to another person.

§2. Concept of Fault

131. In the Uruguayan legislation, Article 1319 of the CC, as was already mentioned, refers to fault but without defining it.

132. Meanwhile, the first paragraph of Article 1344 does define fault by saying that 'Fault is understood as the lack of due care or diligence. It can be gross or mild. Notwithstanding that only one party is interested in a deal, or that it is useful for both of them, it compels the obliged party to behave as a good father of the family, and therefore, to behave with mild fault.'

133. This will lead us to the question: What is the due care or diligence of a good father of a family? This question is answered by Civil law professors, such as Professor Jorge Gamarra,[35] who understands that this is the diligence of an average man; which is not excessively careful, nor excessively careless.

---

33. Article 1382 of the French Civil Code establishes that 'Any act of a person, that causes harm to another, will force he who's fault caused it, to repair it.'
34. This case is commented by Jorge Luis and Jorge Gamarra, in their book 'Responsabilidad Extracontractual', *supra*, p. 22.
35. Jorge Gamarra, 'Tratado de Derecho Civil Uruguayo', Tomo XIX, 2d ed., Editorial Fundación de Cultura Universitaria, Montevideo, 2012.

134. This definition is ratified by Article 1310 of the CC, which regulates the quasi-contract of unofficial agencies and states the following: the unofficial agent is required to employ, in his undertaking, all the care of a good father of the family and will be responsible for the harm caused by the owner, due to his fault or negligence.

135. Finally, Article 18 of the Uruguayan Criminal Code (CP) states that an act is considered as at fault, 'when in order to carry it out, which in itself is legally irrelevant, it causes an outcome that, even though it could have been foreseen, it was not, due to imprudence, inexperience, negligence or infringement of laws or regulations. The outcome that was not wanted, but that was foreseen, is considered intentional; the act that was foreseen as impossible is considered at fault'.

136. Therefore, civil and criminal law include negligence as a behaviour that turns an act into an act at fault. Also, it can be stated that the reference to a good father of the family only applies to civil cases. Criminal law judges analyse the specific case without comparing it with an ideal model. According to Professor Gamarra – citing Planiol – 'fault is the infringement of a preexisting duty'.[36]

137. Therefore, to establish the existence of fault in a specific case, in the first place, it will be necessary to determine the law, regulation or duty that was infringed. It is also a fault when a person acts against the rules that impose a certain conduct, in order not to cause harm to others. There will also be a fault when a person acts against the general duty that imposes that all individuals that live in society behave with the diligence of a good father of the family, which can be understood as the duty to behave without imprudence, without negligence and without inexperience.[37]

138. Another question to be made regarding fault is the following: Does this duty cover all persons? And the answer is no. This duty will be enforceable only regarding the people who are close and who can be directly affected by the acts of the offender (the neighbour principle).

139. Regarding this issue, Gamarra, in his treaty, quotes Prosser who, in his book *Torts*, comments on the *Palsgraf* case, in which judge Cardoso ruled in favour of the defendant. In this case, which happened in the United States, the defendant was a railway employee who helped a passenger climb into the train while it was already moving, and due to this act, a package of this passenger fell into the tracks. It is the case that this package contained fireworks, which when exploded, harmed Mrs Helen Palsgraf. Due to the fact that this person, when the negligence occurred, was situated far from the zone of danger, the judge understood that the employee

36. Planiol, T. II, n. 863, p. 273, quoted by Gamarra, 'Tratado de Derecho Civil Uruguayo', Tomo XIX, *supra*, p. 101.
37. Gamarra, 'Tratado de Derecho Civil Uruguayo', Tomo XIX, *supra*, p. 113.

acted with negligence regarding the passenger, but not regarding Mrs Palsgraf and, therefore, was not responsible for the harm suffered by Mrs Palsgraf.[38]

§3. Duty of Care

140. The duty of care is established in Article 1319 of the CC when it establishes that 'Every unlawful act of men that causes harm to another, imposes to the individual who's wilful misconduct, fault or negligence has generated the harm, the duty to repair it.' The authors understand that this article establishes the duty not to harm others and also determines a sanction in case of doing so.

141. Also, as was pointed out before, Uruguayan law establishes a general duty that imposes that all individuals that live in the society must behave with the diligence of a good father of the family, which can be understood as the duty to behave without imprudence, without negligence, and without inexperience.

§4. Capacity (Infants, Minors)

142. Article 1320 of the CC states the general rule regarding the capacity to commit a crime or a quasi-crime, saying that 'no one with less than ten years, or with a mental illness, can commit a crime, but in case the persons that were in charge of them acted with negligence, they shall take responsibility for the damage caused'.

143. According to Professor Gamarra, only the person that has the psychological aptitude to commit an act can be held responsible for it. Therefore, people with mental illness and those with less than 10 years of age do not have this psychological aptitude to respond to their actions.[39]

---

38. Prosser, Torts, n. 43, pp. 254–255; Fleming, An introduction, p. 49; quoted by Gamarra, 'Tratado de Derecho Civil Uruguayo', Tomo XIX, *supra*, pp. 113–114.
39. Gamarra, 'Tratado de Derecho Civil Uruguayo', Tomo XIX, *supra*, p. 143.

Chapter 2. Specific Cases of Liability

§1. Liability of Professionals

I. In General: Higher Statutory Standard of Care for 'Experts'

144. Law 17.250 does not only legislate about product liability but also regulates the liability for the provision of services. Even though Article 5 of this law distinguishes any product from any service, this law treats them equally and unifies the regime that, without doubt, is of strict liability. The only exception for this regime is the case of liberal professionals who assume obligations of means (and not results). The first problem in this law is that it is much more difficult to establish a defective service than it is to establish a defective product.

145. The Uruguayan Civil Code (CC) also regulates this matter. Therefore, regarding the liability of professionals, there are two regimes of liability: on the one hand, the breach of contract, when the professional does not perform, or performs inaccurately, the services he is obliged to provide (Article 1342 of the CC) and the responsibility created by Article 34 of Law 17.250, which refers to the execution of a service with a material damage (harm to the physical integrity or to the property of the consumer).

146. According to Professor Gamarra, the scope of applicability of Article 34 of Law 17.250 is limited to the cases of the provision of services that imply risk, danger or damage.[40] Therefore, in cases in which the service provided does not imply risk, danger or damage, Article 1342 of the CC will apply.

147. This article states the following: 'the debtor is condemned to the compensation of damages, due to the breach of contract, or to the delay in the execution, even though the debtor did not act with bad faith, as long and he does not justify the breach in a strange cause not attributable to him'.

148. Although Uruguayan doctrine asserts that a professional's liability should be measured through the standard of a good businessman, the law only states for all cases, that the standard to be taken into account is that of a good family father; therefore, this average standard of diligence should be the one applicable to professionals, taking into account, the characteristics of each case.

149. An exception to this is Article 83 of Law 16.060, which states that administrators and representatives of legal entities must act with royalty and with the diligence of a good businessman. Therefore, the main rule to analyse a professional's liability (as long as he has not agreed to obtain a result) will be Article 1344 of the CC, which states that: 'Fault is understood as the lack of due care or diligence. It can be gross or mild. Notwithstanding that only one party is interested in the deal,

40. Jorge Gamarra, 'Responsabilidad Extracontractual', Tomo XX, 2d ed., Editorial Fundacion Cultura Universitaria, Montevideo, 2012, p. 147.

or that it is useful for both of them, it holds the obliged party responsible to behave as a good father of family, and therefore, to behave with mild fault.'

150. Regarding this article, Civil law author Gustavo Ordoqui understands that the liability of professionals must be appreciated, taking into account the diligence required in Article 1344, which considers guilt the lack of care or diligence, and this obligation is more or less intense depending on the nature of the contract or the group of circumstances (…).

151. It is not correct to say that the professional has a more demanding standard of care. The standard is different according to the model of behaviour that is used to qualify the acts performed, taking into account his qualities, personal attitude and the circumstances of the case. There is not a concept of guilt different from the professional – patient or – client relationship. What happens is that in order to weigh which has to be the behaviour of a good professional, it is not taken into account the conduct of a good father or a good businessman but of a good professional. This is the requirement which considers what would have been the normal way of acting of a professional with the same characteristics that had the same knowledge and that had acted with prudence, skills, diligence and dedication, considering the circumstances of time and place.[41]

II. Medical Practitioners

152. In Uruguay, jurisprudence understands that medical practitioners are not obliged to heal the sick but to dedicate their careful, prudent and technical assistance in the degree consistent with the evolution of science.[42]

153. Therefore, for Uruguayan judges, the behaviour to be expected of the medical practitioners is one of prudence and diligence. For a medical practitioner to be liable, it is required that he acts with guilt, which must be proved by the patient. The duty of a medical practitioner is a duty where he is not obliged to obtain results.[43]

154. Civil authors understand that a medical practitioner cannot promise a result, because his powers are limited. Medicine is an inaccurate science and, therefore, in the case of a patient with certain symptoms, several medical practitioners can diagnose differently.[44]

---

41. Ordoqui, Gustavo, 'Responsabilidad Civil del Abogado y del Escribano', Editorial Universidad Católica, Montevideo, 2007, pp. 80–82.
42. Uruguayan Supreme Court Ruling Nº 141/2001 dated 3 Aug. 2001.
43. Jorge Gamarra, 'Responsabilidad Civil Médica', Tomo I, Editorial Fundación de Cultura Universitaria, Montevideo, 2000, pp. 9–12.
44. Jorge Gamarra, 'Responsabilidad Civil Médica', Tomo I, *supra*, p. 15.

155. Another issue that is considered by Uruguayan doctrine is the one called *iatrogenia*, or medical risk. It refers to the fact that, sometimes, medical practitioners might hurt the patient while trying to cure them. For example, a medical surgery will cause pain to the patient; some medicines might generate physical discomfort, etc.

156. Therefore, *iatrogenia* is defined as the injury or sickness produced by the medical practitioner through the exercise of his profession in a correct and guiltless way. And this is explained by the imperfection of medicine, the insecurity of medical acts, the predispositions of the patient, the state of necessity, and it has even been said that *iatrogenia* is the Act of God of medicine.[45]

157. Notwithstanding the aforesaid, there is a part of the Uruguayan doctrine and jurisprudence that understands that, in some cases, medical acts are not uncertain (such as in very simple surgical operations) and, therefore, in these cases, we will be before an obligation of results and not merely of means.

158. Medical liability is regulated by the general principles of law and, therefore, to this liability, Articles 1344,[46] 1319[47] and 1324[48] of the CC will apply, as well as Article 18 of the Criminal Code.[49] This is due to the fact that in Uruguay, medical practice is not regulated by a specific law.

159. Applying Article 1344 to the case in hand, it could be established that the medical practitioner: (i) has the duty to act with diligence; (ii) this diligence must be the average diligence required; (iii) the lack of diligence is equivalent to guilt;

---

45. Achával, 'Responsabilidad Civil del Médico', 2º Edición, Buenos Aires, 1996, pp. 107–111, cited by Jorge Gamarra, in 'Responsabilidad Civil Médica', Tomo I, *supra*, p. 18–19.
46. Article 1344 of the Civil Code states: 'Fault is understood as the lack of due care or diligence. It can be gross or mild. Notwithstanding that only one party is interested in signing the deal, or that it is useful for both of them, it holds the obliged party responsible to behave as a good father of family, and therefore, to behave with mild fault (…).'
47. Article 1319 of the Civil Code states: 'Every unlawful act of men that cause harm to another, imposes to the individual who's wilful misconduct, fault or negligence has generated the harm, the duty to repair it. When the unlawful act has been performed with wilful misconduct, that is, with intent to harm, it constitutes a crime, when the will to harm is missing; the unlawful act constitutes a quasi-crime. In one case and in the other, the unlawful act can be negative or positive, depending this on the duty infringed, and if it referred to a duty to do, or to refrain from doing.'
48. Article 1324 states: 'There is a duty to repair, not only the damage caused directly, but also the damage caused due to acts of one's dependents or by the things that one uses or has to take care of. (…)This liability will cease, when the people mentioned above proofs that they employed all of the diligence of a good family father, in order to avoid the damage.'
49. Article 18 of the Criminal Code points out that: No one can be punished for an act that the law foresees as a crime, if it is not intentional, ultra intentional or guilty, and performed with conscience and will. The act is considered intentional, when the result adjusts to the intent, ultra intentional when the result surpasses the intent, as long as that result could have been foreseen, and guilty when, wanting to perform an act, in itself legally indifferent, a result occurs that, even though it could have been foreseen, it was not, due to the recklessness, inexperience, negligence or violation of laws or regulations. The result that was not wanted, but that was foreseen, is considered intentional, the damage that was deemed as impossible is considered guilty. In no case can an unlawful result be punished if it was different or more serious that the one desired, and could not been foreseen by the agent.

(iv) the guilt makes the medical practitioner incur in liability; and (v) this liability must be appreciated in a case-by-case basis.

160. Article 1344 does not establish degrees of guilt and, therefore, it is understood that the medical practitioner will be liable whenever they do not act with the diligence of a family father.[50]

III. Legal Practitioners

161. According to Article 146 of Act 15.750 (Organic Law of the Judiciary and Organization of Courts), 'lawyers are liable before their clients regarding any damage that can be legally attributable to them'.

162. Therefore, in virtue of this article, and Articles 1344, 1319 and 1324 of the CC, as well as Article 18 of the Criminal Code, already mentioned, lawyers will have to compensate for the damage caused to their clients, whenever it is proved that they did not act with the average of diligence required by law (diligence of a father of the family).

163. Notwithstanding this, it is important to point out that legal practitioners can act in a legal procedure only as advisors of their clients or also as representatives of them.

164. This faculty is established in Article 44 of the General Procedure Code in which it is stated that:

> *44.*1 At any stage of the procedure, before any authority with jurisdictional power, unless in case of a criminal matter, the signing attorney, in its capacity of sponsor of the party, besides the faculties of Article 143 of the Organic Law of the Judiciary and Organization of Courts (Law no. 15.750, dated June 24, 1985), and as long as it is agreed through writing or judicial minute, the lawyer can be vested, especially and only for that procedure, with the role of judicial representative, with all the procedural faculties, except those that imply the disposition of substantial rights.

165. The lawyer that also acts as a representative has the right to charge more to his client and also assumes more risks. Indeed, regarding the liability of legal practitioners, the Supreme Court of Justice, in its ruling 74/1999 dated 14 April 1999, stated that:

> the common representative, such as the person with power of attorney, is liable for the payment of the costs and court costs of the proceeding, jointly with their

50. Jorge Gamarra, 'Responsabilidad Civil Médica', Tomo I., *supra*, pp. 31–32.

client. (…) That is, the position of the lawyer that only assists and the one that also represents, are not equivalent, and the latter is equivalent, in this sense, to the one of the representative.

IV. Builders and Architects

166. Article 1327 of the CC establishes that:

> The owner of a building is liable for the damage that its wreckage causes, if it is due to the omission of the necessary repairs, or due to the lacking in other way, of the due care that a good father of family would have had. If the wreckage came from a defect of construction, the victim can only repeat against the architect that directed the construction of the building, according to what establishes Chapter II, Title IV, Second Part of this Book (Article 1844).

167. Meanwhile, Article 1844 of the CC states that:

> the architect and the businessman of a building are liable during ten years, if it wrecks partially or totally, due to a defect in its construction, of due to a defect in the land, or due to the bad quality of materials, even when the owner had provided or not the materials, and even when there is an exoneration clause. The statute of limitations will be of ten years, which will start when the building was delivered, but after the defect is manifested, the plaintiff will have the time of the personal actions (which is of ten years). The regulation of the first paragraph will apply, unless the architect or businessman, proof the contrary.
>
> This article was changed by Law 19.726, which applies to construction contracts signed after 2019. The new regulation states that:
>
> The architect, the engineer, the constructor and the businessman of a building destined to last for a long time, will be liable for ten years, for the defects or flaws which, entirely or partially, affect the stability or structural strength or prevent its use in the way agreed expressly or tacitly, or prevent its use in the way the building would normally be used, due to a defect of the construction or the land, an incorrect site management, calculation defects, or due to the bad quality of materials, supplied or not by the contracting party, and even in the presence of an exculpatory clause, being this regulation mandatory.
>
> The architect, the engineer, the constructor and the businessman can only exonerate from this liability if they prove that the flaw or defect was caused by a strange cause, not attributable to them.
>
> The defect in the materials supplied by the contracting party is not considered a strange cause, even if they were not rejected. This will not be considered a strange cause, even if the damage was caused during the execution.
>
> For the other defects or flaws, except the ones which only affect the termination elements or construction finishes, the architect, engineer, constructor and businessman will be liable for five years. For the defects of flaws which only affect termination elements or construction finishes, the liability will last

for two years. In these cases, the exoneration from liability can refer to any strange cause not attributable to those individuals.

The liability referred to previously, will be assumed not only regarding the contracting party, but also the following buyers of the building.

The terms in which the claim can be made are the ones pointed out previously, and will begin at the time of the reception of the work. Once the action arises, because the flaw or defect appears, the statute of limitations is of four years.

168. Gamarra understands that this difference between the general regime for contractual liability and the one for liability due to the wreckage of a building is based in the necessity to look after the safety of the individuals. But also, it seeks to protect the interest of the person who hires the construction of the building, because only after a period of time has passed it is possible to know if the building was constructed properly.[51]

169. Because of this, the article establishes a period of time (or of warranty) which has a duration of ten years, which starts running when the building is delivered. If the defect reveals within this period, the architect or the businessman who built it will be liable. Conversely, after the period of ten years (or four years for contracts signed after 13 January 2019) has passed, without any defects being detected, the contractor will stop being liable. This period has given the name to this type of liability, which, in Uruguay, is called the Decennial Liability.

170. Regarding the other characteristics of this liability, it is the same as the common regime of contractual liability. It is based on the guilt of the businessman or architect who built the building. Therefore, if the victim proves the use of faulty materials in the construction or a defect in the land or in the construction, then the defendant can only liberate from liability by proving that this happened due to a strange cause, not attributable to him.

171. Doctrine has understood that the notion of a building must be understood in a wide sense, comprising bridges, dykes, machines, roads, etc. Not all defects are included in this regulation, but only those which are hidden at the time of the delivery of the building. Therefore, if, at the time of the delivery of the building, there are evident defects and the contracting party accepts it with those defects (although the law allows him to refuse to accept it), then it will be understood that the contracting party accepts these defects, which waves his right to complain about them.

172. Notwithstanding this, after the enactment of Law 17.250 (enacted on 11 August 2000), if the contracting party is a final consumer, he has the right to file a claim even regarding the evident defects of the building and even after receiving the building without observations, because this law comprises the construction contracts.

51. Jorge Gamarra, 'Tratado de Derecho Civil Uruguayo', Tomo I, Editorial FCU, Montevideo, 1995, p. 286.

173. This law establishes a statute of limitations of ninety days to complain regarding these apparent defects referred to long-lasting products or services. Regarding the legal standing to sue the architect or constructor of a building, for its wreckage, authors, such as Gamarra, understand that if the contracting party sells the property to another person, they must agree on a conventional subrogation of this action because, if they do not, then the purchaser of the building will only have the action stated on Article 1726 of the CC (action of six months)[52] and the action of Law 17.250 for hidden defects, which also is of six months for the defect to appear, and after it appears, the purchaser will have three months to file a claim. This problem was solved by Law 19.726, which provided that the buyers of the building will also have the right to file a claim in the terms of Article 1844.

174. If the contractor and the architect are condemned to pay compensation, each of them will have to pay proportionately to their liability in the defect. If it is not possible to establish this liability, then both will have to pay half of the compensation (they are not jointly liable).[53]

175. While the aforesaid refers to a contractual liability, Article 1327 refers to an extra-contractual liability (third parties harmed by a building can claim a compensation for the damages to the owner or to the builder, depending on the cause of the harm). Regarding this liability, Professor Peirano Facio has understood that we are before a kind of strict liability.[54] Gamarra, however, understands that this is a case of presumed guilt because it refers to the liability for the act of things and, therefore, Article 1324 applies.

176. According to this article, the victim must file a claim against the owner of the building, if: (i) the wreckage occurred due to the omission of necessary repairs; or if (ii) it happened because he did not act with the diligence of a good family father. Meanwhile, if the wreckage occurs due to a construction defect, then the architect or the contractor will be liable for the damage suffered, as long as it occurred within ten years after the delivery of the building.[55]But if the construction contract was signed after 13 January 2019, then the architect, engineer, constructor and businessman will be liable for a period of four years after the defect arises (as long as it appears within the period of time mentioned above).

177. Regarding this liability, it has also been discussed in the Uruguayan doctrine about the scope of the word 'wreckage' mentioned in Article 1327. Some authors and judges understand that wreckage comprises construction defects in the building, while others understand that defects that cause excessive maintenance expenses would also be included in the scope of wreckage.

---

52. Jorge Gamarra, 'Tratado de Derecho Civil Uruguayo', Tomo I, *supra*, pp. 288–289.
53. *Ibid.*, pp. 291–292.
54. Jorge Peirano Facio, 'Responsabilidad Extracontractual', Editorial Barreiro Ramos, Montevideo, 1954, p. 633.
55. Gamarra, 'Tratado de Derecho Civil Uruguayo', Tomo I, *supra*, pp. 293–294.

178. It has also been discussed whether the future owner of a house or apartment who is purchasing the property in instalments (and not the current owner, nor the person who hired the architect for the construction of the building) has the right to sue the architect and the owner of the building, in application of Article 1844 of the CC.

179. In a case in which the future owners of an apartment filed a claim against the architects alleging their liability for the construction defects, the District Court ruled in favour of the plaintiffs and ordered the defendants to pay the amount necessary for the repair of the construction defects, plus USD 5,000 for the pain and suffering damages.

180. The defendants filed an appeal, and the Appellate Court, in its ruling 358/2011 dated 30 November 2011, established that:

> the Court does not share the position of professor Gamarra, who understands that the only person with a right to file a claim in application of Article 1844 is the person who ordered the construction. It also does not share the opinion that the notion of building wreckage to which numeral 2 of Article 1327 refers has the meaning the appellant party attributes to it.

181. Regarding the legal standing to file a claim for liability based on Article 1844 of the CC, the court agrees with the opinion of Doctor Santiago Carnelli about this issue, who affirms that the future owner of real estates, who has already purchased it and is paying for it in instalments, with the promise of the property registered or not, even though is not the person that requested the construction of the building, has a legal standing to file a claim of liability based on Article 1844 of the CC because, due to the fact that he is the one injured by the wreckage of the building, caused by a defect in its construction, numeral 2 of Article 1327 of the CC gives him legal standing to claim against the constructor and/or the architect, by the same regime of the one who orders the construction, regulated by Article 1844 of the CC.[56]

182. Regarding the notion of 'wreckage of the building' to which Article 1327 of the CC refers, the court shares the broad criterion that has followed our jurisprudence, abundantly mentioned in the lawsuit, that the expression is not limited to cases of construction defects that affect the stability of the construction but that it also covers the cases in which the defects turn expensive the maintenance of the building, as a consequence of the infiltration of water through the flat roof, walls or external walls. This is the interpretation proposed by Gamarra, who states that 'our legal regime not only contemplates the case of the total or partial wreckage of the

56. Carnelli, Santiago, 'Titular activo de la responsabilidad decenal y situaciones que la misma abarca', published on ADCU, T. XXVII, págs. 643 a 653.

building that affects its strength or stability, according to Article 1844 of the Civil Code, but also to all other construction defects which are noticed in the building.'[57,58]

V. Others

183. In Uruguay, the professions in which liability is usually analysed are the following: medical practitioners, legal practitioners, notary publics, architects and accountants.

184. Having already analysed the liability of legal and medical practitioners, as well as the liability of architects, we will pass to analyse the liability of notary publics and accountants.

A. Notary Publics

185. In Uruguay, to be a notary public, the professional has to complete the studies of this profession (which is very similar to the career of legal practitioners, but with some differences). There is an Organic Notarial Law which regulates the profession of a notary public. It defines the notary public as 'the person authorized to draft, deliver and authorize under his faith and signature, all the acts and contracts that must be celebrated with his intervention between individuals, or between them and other legal entities'.[59]

186. Article 75 of the Decree 1421 (1878) states that the notary publics will be liable in all cases, before the parties, for the damages they cause due to the bad performance of their functions, notwithstanding the penalties that might correspond.

B. Accountants

187. To be an accountant in Uruguay, the studies related to the career of a certified public accountant must be completed. The liability of the accountant will emerge when he does not possess the theoretical and practical knowledge needed for the practice of his profession and, due to this, causes damages to third parties. The basic functions of accountants are the following:

- to give his opinion regarding the accounting activity performed;
- to advise or deliver consultations and reports;
- to certify accounting statements.[60]

---

57. Gamarra, Jorge,'Tratado de Derecho Civil Uruguayo', T. I, 1957, p. 216.
58. *Bueno, Carlos and other v. Aguerre, Leonardo and other*. Damages. IUE 2-21442/2009. TAC 6, No. 358/2011 (11/30/2011).
59. Ordoqui Castilla, Gustavo, 'Responsabilidad Civil del Profesional Liberal', Editorial Fundación de Cultura Universitaria, 1st ed., Montevideo, 1993, pp. 183–184.
60. Ordoqui Castilla, 'Responsabilidad Civil del Profesional Liberal', *supra*, p. 235.

§2. Liability of Public Authorities

188. Article 24 of the Constitution of the Republic of Uruguay states that:

> The State, the Departmental Governments, the Autonomous Entities, the Decentralized Services, and, in general, every body of the State, will be civilly liable for the damage caused to third parties, in the execution of their public services, entrusted to their management or direction.

189. Meanwhile, Article 25 states that:

> When the damage is caused by the State employees (public servants), in the exercise of their functions, or in occasion of this exercise, in case of having acted with gross negligence or with malice, the public authority in charge can repeat against them, whatever it has paid as compensation.

190. It is important to point out that the Constitution of 1952 modified the regime of State liability, which was double and which admitted action against the public servant. After this modification, the direct liability of the State is established, with the following guarantees: (i) to the public (solvency, not requiring a distinction between the lack of service and the personal fault, etc.); (ii) to the public servants (who will not be disturbed during the performance of their management and will not have to answer but to the State, unless in cases of malice or gross negligence); and (iii) for the State (because it has the possibility, or not, to repeat to the public servant in the cases mentioned, control the management, etc.).[61]

191. One of the most important administrative law authors, Professor Enrique Sayagués Laso, points out that:

> The constitutional text is clear regarding the fact that the patrimonial liability before third parties falls on the Administration, not being possible to bring a lawsuit against the public servant. Besides, this is the only point regarding which it is possible to invoke the parliamentary records, which are clear and explicit in this sense through the different formulas considered. Even more, it was the decisive reason of the reform.[62]

192. Another author that writes about this issue is Daniel Hugo Martins, who mentions the following: 'The liability regulated by Article 24 of the Constitution gathers the following characteristics: is civil, pecuniary, belongs to public law, for administrative acts or incidents, (…) autonomous, primary, anonymous, specific

---

61. Ruling 876/2013 dated 11 Dec. 2013, issued by the Fifth Civil Appelate Court of Uruguay.
62. Enrique Sayagués Laso, 'Tratado de Derecho Administrativo', 6ª ed. puesta al día 1988, Ed. Facultad de Derecho y Ciencias Sociales de la Universidad de la República y Fundación de Cultura Universitaria, Tomo I, p. 659.

and general (…).'[63] This author also explains that the civil nature does not imply that the liability is ruled by the laws of private law but is applied as an opposite to political, criminal or administrative liability to indicate that it is translated into a pecuniary compensation, and it is autonomous, due to the fact that it is regulated by the rules of public law. It is primary, because it allows the direct action of the victim against the State, and is anonymous because it does not require identifying the liable agent; it suffices with the bad functioning or lack of functioning of the service.[64]

193. Afterwards, this author, regarding the liability of the public servants, points out that:

> it is established in Article 25 of the Constitution. This article determines that the public servant is only civilly liable before the Administration. This is one of the principal innovations of the reform of 1951 regarding this matter (…) The first premise of the new regime consists in that the public servants cannot be hold liable by individuals for the damages they cause during the performance of their administrative functions. This is the inverse system from the one established in the Constitution of 1934, in which the public servant was directly liable (…) the second characteristic of this regime consists in the fact that the public body from which the public servant depends, can repeat against him what it had paid as compensation, when he had caused this damage acting with malice, or gross negligence.[65]

194. The Fifth Civil Appellate Court, on its ruling 876/2013 dated 11 December 2013, in a case in which the plaintiffs sued a public employee of the State Health Administration (hereinafter ASSE), stated the following: Indeed, it is very surprising that in the case, neither the parties nor the court in the previous stage, noticed that the hypothesis installed in the case does not fit in the field of contractual or extra-contractual liability of private law, but is referred to a case against ASSE and one of its employees, which, – before third parties who suffered damages – would eventually involve the direct and exclusive liability of the State, but not of the public servant.

195. Regarding Dr Sosa (the public servant), the plaintiffs did not refer to other different relationships from the one of public law which, in the constitutional and legal sphere, does not allocate legal standing to the public servant but to the public entity, which is the only person to whom a claim can be filed directly, by who alleges to have been damaged. (…)

63. Daniel Hugo Martins, Constitución y Administración', Ed. Industria Gráfica Nuevo Siglo Ltda., Montevideo, 1993, p. 235.
64. Martins, Constitución y Administración, *supra*, pp. 230, 235.
65. *Ibid.*, p. 251.

§3. Abuse of Rights

196. Article 1321 of the CC states that 'he who uses his rights does not harm others'. This article is not precise due to the fact that sometimes a person using a right causes harm to others. An example of this is a person who operates a gym in a residential neighbourhood. This will bring traffic and customers that are unknown to the neighbours, cars will generate the reduction of parking spaces, etc. Nevertheless, if it is legal to operate a gym in that zone, then the gym's owner will be acting according to law and, therefore, will not be liable for the nuisance caused.

197. Therefore, the correct assertion would be to say that the harm produced as a consequence of the exercise of a right is protected by a ground of justification (to act according to law), which exonerates his author.[66] Therefore, harm will be caused, but this damage will not be subject to compensation. Notwithstanding this, abuse of rights can happen when there is a deviation in the exercise of the right (regarding the interest pursued or the modality of its exercise).

198. Doctrine distinguishes between abuse of rights in contractual and in extra-contractual law: In contractual law, Professors Jorge Luis and Jorge Gamarra state that one case of abuse of rights can be the one referred to as the duty to act with good faith. Indeed, Article 1291 of the CC states that contracts must be carried out by the parties with good faith. Therefore, good faith is a boundary in the exercise of the rights derived from the contract,[67] and if this boundary is breached, then we will be before a case of abuse of rights.

199. There are articles in the CC that expressly order compensation in case of a breach of the obligation of good faith. Indeed, Article 1933 of the Civil Code states that a partner of a civil society must quit 'in good faith and in timely fashion' because, in case he does not do this, he will have to pay damages.

§4. Injury to Reputation and Privacy

200. In Uruguay, the right to reputation and privacy is not consecrated. Nevertheless, the doctrine and the jurisprudence understand that there are two articles in the Constitution that consecrate these rights. Article 7 of the Constitution states that 'The inhabitants of the Republic have the right to be protected in the enjoyment of their life, honour, liberty, security, job and property. No one can be deprived of these rights except according to the laws which are established for reasons of general interest.'

---

66. Gamarra & Gamarra, 'Responsabilidad Extracontractual', *supra*, p. 24.
67. Franzoni, Degli effectti del contratto, p. 270, cited by Gamarra & Gamarra, 'Responsabilidad Extracontractual', *supra*.

201. While Article 72 states that: 'the list of rights, duties and guarantees stated by the Constitution, does not exclude the other which are inherent to the human personality, or are derived from the republican form of government'.

202. Indeed, Professor Gamarra, regarding the right to intimacy, points out the following:

> Going out to the street determines that it cannot be alleged a right to intimacy, because this right is only conceivable in the private life, but from this it cannot be deduced that the person loses all his right to his image, because this right is not indissolubly linked to his reserved or secret life, neither does it confuses with it … Besides, the exceptions that we have referred to, does not imply that when a person acts in public he is tacitly waiving his right to his image (because this is a fiction) but that the law solved this conflict between an individual interest and the general interest of the public knowledge or of the information, giving priority to the second one. Therefore, the right to the personality of the portrayed person will only be sacrificed, when the social purpose of the information has to prevail over it.[68]

203. While the constitutional law Professor Martin Risso has stated the following:

> The right to the image is configured as a right of the personality, derived from the human dignity and aims to protect the moral dimension of people, which attributes to his owner a right to determine the graphic information generated by his personal physical features, which can have public diffusion. The power granted by this right, as a fundamental right, mainly consists in preventing the obtaining, reproduction or publication of ones image by a third party not authorized, without mattering which is the purpose – for information, commercial, scientific, cultural, etc. – of the person that captures or broadcasts it.[69]

204. Regarding Uruguayan jurisprudence in this matter, the Fourth Civil Court of Appeals, in its Ruling no. 39, dated 28 February 2012, in a case in which the plaintiffs asked for compensation for non-pecuniary damages after they were filmed in the parliament trying to separate two persons who were fighting, which was used for an advertisement of condoms, established the following.

205. 'In the lawsuit it is claimed compensation for the damages suffered due to the unduly use of the image of the plaintiffs, in an advertisement of the condoms *Preventor*. The plaintiffs are public servants of the Legislative Power, and they appear in the filming trying to separate the protagonists of a fight, occurred in the Representatives Chamber; after the showing of this filming, an image appears with

---

68. Jorge Gamarra, Anuario de Derecho Civil Uruguayo, Tomo XIII, Montevideo, p. 115.
69. Martin J. Risso Ferrand, 'Algunas reflexiones sobre los derechos al honor, a la intimidad, a la propia imagen y la libertad de prensa', Biblioteca Jurídica Virtual del Instituto de Investigaciones Jurídicas de la UNAM.

the phrase "for a more relaxed world"; this advertisement was broadcasted by Channel 10 in central time, and afterwards it was removed, but it is still being broadcasted in the web page of the company, and the video can still be found in youtube.'

206. From the elements that provide conviction, which were introduced, it can be inferred that the public servants' image was used, they were in a public place and this was performed without their authorization and for commercial purposes.

207. The right to the image is a fundamental right, explicitly acknowledged by the Constitution of the Republic, due to the fact that it is a right inherent to human personality (Article 72) (…).

208. Article 21 of Act No. 9739 (Author Rights law) states that the portrait of a person cannot be used commercially without his express consent. In this law, it is stated that a portrait can be published when it is related to scientific, teaching and, in general, cultural purposes or with facts or events of public interest or that have been performed in public.

209. 'In its analysis, although the public servants were located in a public place, the broadcasting of the images did not have scientific, teaching or cultural purposes; neither did they broadcast in an event of public interest. Within this last notion, it can be understood the broadcasting of the fight in the Representatives Chamber, in the news or journalism programmes, but in this case the image was used in an advertisement, without authorization and accompanied by an ironic message, which exposed the plaintiffs to mockery … .'

210. 'In virtue of the aforementioned, it must be concluded that the defendant, when she broadcasted the image of the plaintiffs, without their consent, with commercial purposes (not with the purpose of informing neither with scientific, cultural or informative purposes), incurred in an unlawful act that caused a damage that must be repaired.'

I. Non-pecuniary Damage for the Illegitimate Use of the Image

211. In the aforementioned case, the court, in reference to pain and suffering damages, stated the following:

> 'Regarding the extra patrimonial damage, the Court has expressed in previous rulings that:
>
> the existence of pain and suffering should be analyzed according to the general criteria in the matter of extra-contractual liability, due to the fact that the law in analysis (Law 9.739, which regulates author rights) does not establish a special liability regime.

212. As has been sustained by the court, the principle in this matter is that the non-pecuniary damage must be proved by the person that alleges its existence and its amount, according to general principles (Articles 137, 139, 140 of the C.G.P.), notwithstanding the use of simple presumptive elements that admit proof in contrary (…).

213. And in this case, (…) it had been proved that the defendants have incurred in an unlawful behaviour and that the plaintiffs have suffered spiritual trouble as a consequence of the mockeries and jokes that generated the broadcasting of the filming, especially in the labour environment.

214. Regarding the amount of the sentence, this was not reviewed because it adjusts to the parameters normally appealed by the court (the court condemned each of the defendants to pay USD 2,500 plus 6% of annual interest since the date on which the unlawful act happened).

215. In another case, in which the defendant was accused of theft, the Second Criminal Appeal Court established the following:

> the defendant alleges that the recording filed in Court was taken in violation of the right to intimacy, and therefore, is an illegal proof. It is clear that the right to intimacy is the manifestation of the freedom of a person, of which several of its manifestations are protected by criminal law … . Intimacy is understood as the personal sphere in which a person, preserved from the outside world, can increase the possibilities to develop and promote his personality … But to this we must add the control that necessarily the person has to exercise over these activities or personal attitudes that constitute his intimacy … , this way, if the person never had or lost the possibility to control the diffusion of certain acts or circumstances affecting him, then this diffusion is not punishable.

216. Mantovani, agreeing with this point of view, establishes two groups of behaviours that threaten intimacy: acts of indiscretion and acts of revelation.

217. The first one imply to take knowledge of something that happens in the private sphere of the person, whether it is by: (a) direct penetration (breaking into his home); (b) indirect penetration (zoom lens, microphones, etc.); (c) interference in the mass media (interception of mails, phone calls); and (d) through investigations of the life of others (parents, spouse, children, etc.) (…).

218. In this case, there was nothing related to the right to intimacy due to the fact that what was recorded was not being referred to his intimacy, but to the bad economic situation of the accuser (…).

219. In conclusion, in this aspect, the court understands that ‘the appellant is not right, because the proof files cannot be deemed illegal’.

II. Reputation

220. Finally, regarding the right to reputation, the Criminal Code, in its Article 179, when referring to false accusations, states that:

> He who knowingly, accuses someone before the judicial or police authority, or before the Advising Committee in Economic and Finance Matters of the State, or before a public servant who has the duty to inform to these authorities, a crime that has not been committed, or that creates the signs of a crime, so that a criminal proceeding is started for its investigation, will be sentenced from three months of prison to three years of penitentiary.

221. While Article 333 of the Criminal Code, regarding the crime of libel, states that:

> he who, before several persons gathered or separately, but in a way that can be disseminated, attributed to a person a specific fact, that, if being true, could give place against him to a criminal or disciplinary proceeding, or expose him to the public hate or disdain, will be sentenced from four years of prison, to three years of penitentiary, or to a fine from 80 to 800 adjustable units.

222. Afterwards, in Article 334, when referring to slander, the Criminal Code establishes that:

> He who, outside of the aforesaid cases, offended in any way, with words, writs or acts, the honor, the righteousness or the decorum of a person, will be sentenced to three to eighteen months of prison, or a fine from 60 to 400 adjustable units.

223. Article 335 of the Criminal Code states, as aggravating circumstances, which will imply the increase of the sentence by one-sixth of it, that these crimes are committed in public instruments or with writs, drawings or paintings publicly broadcasted or exposed to the public.

224. While Article 336 of the Criminal Code states that there will be no liability when: (i) the information being told or broadcasted is referred to issues of public interest and relates to public servants or persons that, due to their profession or occupation, have a relevant social exposure or to any person that has been involved voluntarily in issues of public interest; (ii) the person reproduces any type of manifestation about issues of public interest, when the author is identified; (iii) when he told or broadcasted any type of humorous or artistic manifestation, as long as it refers to any of the precedent hypothesis.

225. This exemption of liability will not proceed when it is proven the malice of the author and the intent to offend the persons or to damage their private life.

226. The persons accused of the crimes of libel and slander will have the right to prove the truth of the facts and the truthfulness of the qualities attributed to the person, except in the case that this refers to the person's private life or when the broadcasting of these facts is not of public interest. If the truth or plausibility is proven, the author of the act will be exempted from punishment unless he had applied malice.

227. According to Article 338, these crimes are punishable only after the accusation is made by the victim. If he has passed away before making the accusation, but with time to exercise this right, or if the offence was directed to the memory of a deceased, then the accusation can be filed by the spouse or close relatives. In case the offence is directed against a legal entity with social, political or administrative purposes, the accusation can only be made with the authorization of the legal entity.

228. In the case of false accusations, the statute of limitations will be for ten years. In the case of libel, it will be for one year, and in the case of slander, three months.

229. Finally, according to Article 125, the civil action will have the same statute of limitations than the one established for the crime.

230. Regarding Uruguayan jurisprudence, the Supreme Court, in its ruling 146/2006 dated 30 August 2006, stated the following, in a case in which a public servant accused a journalist of a newspaper of libel after he published two articles in which he accused him of fraud and theft: 'It must be concluded that the means or phrases used by the accused are offensive with no good reason, and if it was understood that the facts were serious, he could have informed the population in other terms, and not in the offensive way he did.'

231. One thing is that a public person is subject to the control of the mass media and subject to their review, and the other, very differently, is to offend the reputation of a person, as it happened in the present case. As Langón points out:

> The exception of truth only exempts from punishment inasmuch as the accused did not employ means or phrases offensive with no good reason .... Without good reason means to say something in vain, baseless, excessively, that does not add anything substantive, except the offensive content that the means or expressions used contain (...) (Criminal Code, t. II, page. 318).[70]

70. *AA and BB v. CC* – Press Law (No. 16.099) – Criminal Cassation, IUE 302-188/2004, Supreme Court, No. 146/2006 (08/30/2006).

§5. Interference with Contractual Relations

232. The right to the compliance of a contract is protected internally for the case in which the debtor, with his behaviour, breaches the contract, generating a hypothesis of contractual liability; also, it is protected externally when it is a third party (and not the debtor) who generates the breach of the contract (extra-contractual liability).

233. The second situation became very common in Uruguay, regarding contracts of promises for the sale of real estate, before 1970 (during the time this contract could not be registered).

234. This was a time of great inflation, where it was in the interest of the seller to breach the contract because the inflation had turned the contract into a bad business for him. Therefore, he sold the property to a third party, at a higher price, that compensated for the penalties and damages he had to pay for the breach of contract.

235. In these cases, it could happen that the third party knew about the promise and still, celebrated a contract with the seller, which implied the necessity to breach another contract (damaging, in consequence, the legitimate right of the buyer), or it could have even happened that the third party took the initiative, convincing the debtor to breach the contract. Due to this, the national doctrine and jurisprudence started questioning the lawfulness of these actions.

236. Another case analysed by doctrine is the case in which a person, for example, a construction company, while performing works in the street, damages an electric line, preventing, for some time, the production of a pasta fabric which suffers the loss of profits.

237. The third example analysed is the case in which the debtor of a person is killed by a third party (in a car accident, for example), and due to this, his creditor suffers pecuniary damages (because his credit is not paid).[71]

238. The protection of the credit, in this sense, is defended by some authors, applying Article 1319 of the CC, which states that: 'Every unlawful act of men that causes harm to another, imposes to the individual whose wilful misconduct, fault or negligence has generated the harm, the duty to repair it (…).'

239. Regarding this issue, it is discussed whether this type of action can be analysed in the field of the extra-contractual liability or if it should be located in the contractual area.

240. Some authors understand that the laws referred to contractual liability protect the credit of the creditor and, therefore, there is no need to hold liable someone other than the debtor.

71. Gamarra, 'Tratado de Derecho Civil Uruguayo', Tomo XIX, *supra*, p. 289.

241. This opinion has the flaw that in case the party who breaches the contract is insolvent, then the creditor will not be able to compensate for the damages suffered.

Regarding this matter, Gamarra states that: 'this situation is regulated by article 1319 (of the CCU), and therefore, it admits malice as well as fault (…) and if the guilty behaviour also is punishable, even more will (an unlawful act) exist in the case of bad faith, (which is more intense than the fault). Therefore, the third party who knew (bad faith) or should have known (guilt) about the credit right affected, is liable, even if the initiative of the second contract was not his (but of the debtor), because in any case he is helping the debtor breach his contract, and causes this breach, because without the third party's help, the breach would not have happened'.[72]

This opinion is shared by national jurisprudence. The Seventh Appellate Court, in its ruling 191/07 dated 5 of September of 2007, stated the following:

> 1. As this Court has previously maintained in similar situations (rulings Nos. 161/00, 111/01), a damage in the credit right of a third party occurs, when the unlawful behaviour of the defendant injures the credit right of the plaintiff, (…) and notwithstanding the criteria for the distinction of extra-contractual and contractual liability, this case must be solved with the simple application of the regulations referred to liability for an unlawful act, which has a general application in all the positive law legal system, because the person who causes a harm must repair it (articles 1319, 1342 and concordant of the Civil Code).

§6. Others: Liability for Unsafe Condition of Public Roads

242. According to Article 24 of the Uruguayan Constitution, 'the State, the Departmental Governments, the Autonomous Entities, the Decentralized Services and, in general, any government body, will be civilly liable of the damage caused to third parties, in the execution of the public services trusted to its management or direction'.

243. Taking into account that public roads are considered a public service that the State must provide, their unsafeness would generate the strict liability of the State, even in the case where its construction had been delegated to contractors.

244. Regarding this strict liability, ruling 721/1996 of the Supreme Court of Justice, stated that:

72. *Ibid.*, p. 305.

> For this type of liability to exist, it is necessary that we are before an unlawful act of the Administration, case in which the principle that imposes compensation would apply. And in some cases, even if the act of the Administration is lawful, it has to compensate for it, if the damage caused is exceptional or uncommon.[73]

245. Uruguayan authors also have written about this type of liability. One of the most important administrative lawyers of Uruguay, Professor Sayagues Laso, has pointed out the following:

> The damage suffered must be special, exceptional, surpass the normal sacrifices typical of life in society. If the law affected equally all or a great number of people, i.e., if, in fact, the effects were really general, there would be no obligation to compensate.[74]

---

73. *Bonnet Brignone, Julio Alberto and Amonal S.A. v. Intendencia Municipal de Montevideo*, Extra contractual liability, IUE 310/94, Supreme Court, (07/22/1996).
74. Laso, Tratado de Derecho Administrativo, *supra*, p. 610.

Part II. Liability for the Acts of Others

Chapter 1. Vicarious Liability

§1. Employer/Employee

246. Vicarious liability is regulated by Article 1324 of the CC, which states that:

> There is a duty to repair, not only the damage caused directly, but also the damage caused due to acts of one's dependents or by the things that one uses or has to take care of. This way, parents are responsible for the acts of their children, when they are under parental authority, and live with them; guardians are responsible for the behaviour of the persons that live under their authority and care; school directors and artisans are responsible for the damage caused by their students or apprentices, during the time they are under their watch and, finally, the owners or directors of an establishment or company will be liable for the damage caused by their employees, when providing the service for which they were employed. This liability ceases when the people mentioned above proofs that they employed the diligence of a good family father, in order to avoid the damage.

247. Therefore, according to Uruguayan law, employers will respond for the acts of their employees, when they cause damage while providing the service for which the employer hired them. Most authors commenting on this article state that the employee must act with guilt in order for the employer to be liable, but this is not pointed out in Article 1324.

248. Article 1326 states that:

> those forced to repair the damage caused by their dependents, have the right to be compensated by them with their assets, if they had any, as long as the person that caused the damage did it without any order or knowledge of the person to whom he owed obedience, and as long as he was capable of committing a crime or quasi-crime, according to Article 1320.

249. Therefore, if it turns out that the person that caused the damage is, for example, mentally impaired, then the employer will not be liable for this damage. But if it is proven that the employer knew that this person was mentally impaired, then the employer will be directly liable for hiring someone unfit for the position.

250. For this liability to arise, it is not necessary that the employee that caused the harm be identified. It is only required that the claimant proves that one of the dependents of the certain employer, acting with guilt, caused a damage.[75] Most authors understand that the guilt of the employee is not presumed. The only presumption that this article states is the one referred to the employer, which will have the burden of proof regarding the fact that he acted with the diligence of a good family father in order to avoid the damage that occurred.

251. Notwithstanding this, some District Courts, a Uruguayan Court of Appeal and even the Supreme Court have sustained that the presumption of guilt comprehends also the dependent, arguing that Article 1324, in the end, does not distinguish between employers and employees (it refers to 'the people mentioned above').

252. Proof of the liability: in the cases of liability for acts of others, first, the responsibility of the author of the wrongdoing must be proved. Therefore, in this case, the claimant must prove that the employee acted with guilt, that due to this act, damage was caused, that there is a connection between the wrongdoing and the harm caused and that there is unlawfulness. And the exemptions that can be argued will be the ones of the general regime: the guilt of the victim, third-party responsibility, force majeure or act of God.

253. Usually, the victim of a wrongdoing will file a claim against the employer (in application of Article 1324 of the CC) and against the employee (in application of Article 1319 of the CC, already analysed when referring to the liability regime for one's own acts).

254. If the victim only sues the employee, the employee will not be able to summon the employer in warranty. The reason for this is because the regime operates in favour of the victim, not of the employee.

255. Now, if the victim sues only the employer, the employer can call the employee to trial. This is usually done so that if the employer is condemned to pay compensation, then he will exercise the action of Article 1326 and ask the employee to reimburse this payment.

256. Nevertheless, the ruling against the employee is not a requirement for the court to condemn the employer. This can be explained, among other reasons, by the fact that sometimes the employee cannot be identified.

257. The other question that arises refers to the case in which an employee, with a thing, causes damage to others. This can happen, for example, when the dependent is a driver and runs over a pedestrian.

---

75. Gamarra, 'Tratado de Derecho Civil Uruguayo', Tomo XX, 2d ed., *supra*, p. 217.

258. In this case, the victim will be legitimated to sue the employer: (a) for damage caused by things under the custody of the company; or (b) for the act of a dependent.

259. If the victim sues for both, then we will be before a *cumul*, in which guilt will be presumed, because the dependent was not only dependent but also had the custody of a thing. Uruguayan jurisprudence has accepted the possibility of *cumul* in this case.

§2. Independent Contractors

260. Dependent is not only he who is employed by another but also he who works under the surveillance of others and follows his instructions and complies with a schedule. Independent contractors are those workers that, even though they perform activities for others, do not have a dependency relationship with them. This is the case of a taxi driver, a plumber, an artisan, a car salesman or a mechanic.

261. As regards this point, we deem it relevant to point out that in the past years, laws 18.099 (enacted on 24 January 2007) and 18.251 (enacted on 6 January 2008) were enacted in order to make employers liable for the labour obligations of outsourced companies.

262. Indeed, Article 1 of Law 18.099 establishes that:

> Any employer or business owner who uses subcontractors, intermediaries or workforce suppliers, will be jointly liable for their labour obligations towards the hired employees, as well as for the payment of the social security contributions to the corresponding authority, the premium for the work accident and professional sickness insurance, and for the fines and recoveries owed to the State Insurance Bank, regarding those workers.

263. Therefore, in Uruguay, since 2007, those who outsource are responsible for the payment of labour obligations of their employees as well as for the payment of the obligations of the employees of the companies outsourced. This is why, since then, companies have been controlling the due payments of the employees of the companies outsourced, in order to avoid future claims regarding labour obligations of the latter.

§3. Liability of Legal Entities for Acts of their Organs

264. Regarding the liability of legal entities, such as corporations, limited liability companies, etc., Law 16.060 (called the law of Commercial Societies) has established that when the legal entity organs act on behalf of it, the legal entity will be liable for those actions, as long as some requirements established by law are complied with.

265. The administrators have the administration of the social assets and the management of the businesses comprised in the social object, which is established in the social contract. They must administer the social assets, organize the establishment and the company (internal management) and then perform the activity for which the company was created (external management).

266. For the achievement of all these functions, they must celebrate contracts that will bind the company with third parties, which will be signed by its representatives. The company will be obliged by the acts of its representatives and will only be liable when its representative is acting on its behalf.

267. Sometimes, the same person exercises administration and representation functions. But sometimes, which is the case of the corporations, these functions are performed by different persons: the administrative function is performed by the Board of Directors, and the representation function, according to Law 16.060, will be performed by the President, unless agreed otherwise.

268. For the other types of companies, the division of functions will be expressly provided in the social contract or in a subsequent appointment act. If nothing is said in the contract or in the appointment act, the administrator will be the representative of the company. In Civil law, the administration refers to the conservation of a patrimony, while in commercial law, it includes the capacity to transfer or encumber this patrimony.

269. Article 23 of Law Decree 14.701 (which refers to securities) allows administrators or managers of companies to issue securities on behalf of the company. According to numeral 3 of Article 79 of Law 16.060, the company is obliged by all acts performed by the administrators or representatives of the company that are not blatantly unconnected to the social object.

270. The law supposes that third parties should know what is within and outside the social object of a company, due to the publicity of the contract. If the administrator or representative, acting within the social object, performs activities which are against the law or the social contract or if the act is abusive, that is, attends to their own interest or the interest of a third party, the company will still be obliged to third parties. Notwithstanding this, the administrator or representative will be responsible for their acts before the company.

271. Although an administrator or a board of directors is appointed, associates of a company can reserve, through the contract or in the appointment act, some acts related to the administration of the company. This is established in Articles 207, 240 (final paragraph) and Article 342 of Law 16.060. This will restrain the administrator's faculties. But these restrictions, even when established in the contract, cannot be opposed to third parties.

272. Nevertheless, if the administrator or representative acts in violation of the restraints, he will then be liable before the company. Also, if the third party knew about the restriction and, notwithstanding this, celebrated a contract in violation of the restrictive disposition, then the company will not be obliged to this third party (Article 79, final paragraph of Law 16.060). This rule can be explained by the fact that the law does not want to favour the third party that acts in bad faith.

273. Article 83 of Law 16.060 states that administrators and representatives must act with royalty and with the diligence of a good businessman. The diligence of a good businessman sounds similar to the diligence of the good father of a family, but they are very different.

274. The good father of the family is the person that acts with the carefulness of an average common man. Law 16.060 is more demanding. It is not enough that the administrator or representative acts as an average middleman; he has to act with a special professional ability. To analyse this standard, it is necessary to examine the activity performed by the company. It is not the same to act as an administrator of a bank than to act as a representative of a textile company. Each activity requires different aptitudes and dedication.

275. Loyalty refers to the application of the general principle, which imposes to act with good faith in the execution of the contracts. In the application of this principle, the law establishes some prohibitions: (i) the administrators and representatives cannot celebrate a contract with the company they represent (Article 84 and Article 388 of Law 16.060); (ii) administrators and representatives are forbidden to perform activities competing with the company they represent (Article 85 and Article 389 of Law 16.060); (iii) regarding corporations, there is a special rule that states that the directors of a corporation that have interests which are contrary to the ones of the company, must communicate this circumstance to the board of directors, and should refrain to intervene when these matters are dealt with (Article 387 of Law 16.060).

Chapter 2. Liability of Parents, Teachers and Instructors

276. According to Article 1324 of the CC, there is a duty to repair not only the damage caused directly but also the damage caused due to acts of one's dependents. This way, parents are responsible for the acts of their children when they are under parental authority and live with them. Guardians are responsible for the behaviour of the persons that live under their authority and care, and school directors and artisans are also responsible for the damage caused by their students or apprentices, during the time they are under their watch. This liability will cease when the people mentioned above prove that they employed the diligence of a good family father, in order to avoid the damage.

277. Article 1320 of the CC establishes that 'Neither minors under 10 years, nor mentally impaired are capable of committing a crime or quasi-crime; but the people that are responsible to look after them will be responsible, if they acted with negligence.' This is a case of direct responsibility of a caretaker of the incompetent.

278. It is important to point out that, while Article 1324 presumes the guilt of the incompetent guardian, Article 1320 does not presume it. This is why Gamarra studies these two articles and arrives at the conclusion that Article 1320 refers to the cases in which the caretakers of the incompetents are not the ones established in Article 1324 (i.e., they are not the parent or the legal guardian of the wrongdoer).

279. Professor Gamarra explains this interpretation by saying that when the incompetent commits a crime or quasi-crime while his legal guardian was taking care of him, it is logical that guilt is presumed. Regarding the people to which Article 1320 could refer, Gamarra points out that the relationship between them and the incompetence could be a permanent one or provisional. It could be an uncle, a grandfather or a friend. Another example could be the case in which children go on an excursion organized by their school or the psychiatric patient when confined to a mental institution.[76]

§1. Parents Liability

280. Regarding parents liability, it can be divided into: liability for their own acts and liability for the acts of others. Indeed, if the child who commits the wrongdoing is under ten years, then the parents will answer for their own acts (direct liability), with guilt presumed by Article 1324. While, if the wrongdoing is committed by a minor over ten years and under eighteen years, their parents will be liable for acts of others. In this second case, they will act as guarantors and, therefore, will be before a case of strict liability. It will be necessary to prove the guilt of the minor, but after this is proven, the parents will have to respond as guarantors.

76. *Ibid.*, pp. 311–322.

281. This type of liability is justified in the failure of the parents to watch and educate their children ('guilt *in vigilando* and *in educando*'). Notwithstanding this, authors currently found the basis for this liability in other sources: in the family solidarity, in the policy to prevent guilt and in the guarantee to collect the compensation (when the child is older than ten years, and therefore, is capable of committing a civil crime or quasi-crime).

282. Nevertheless, Article 1326 of the CC establishes that after paying, parents can seek compensation on the patrimony of their child (the wrongdoer). But for this liability to operate, children must be under the parental custody of their parents. Children are under parental custody until they turn eighteen years (Article 280, No. 2 of the CC). Also, for this liability to apply, the child's parents cannot have been suspended from or lost parental custody (Articles 285 and 295 of the CC).

283. Since the enactment of the law dated 18 September 1946 (Article 11), parental custody has been exercised jointly by the child's father and mother. Before this law, the Civil Code established that the father would exercise the parental custody, and in his absence, the child's mother would exercise it. Therefore, nowadays, both the father and the mother will have to respond for the whole compensation (and not for half of it, each).

284. Before the law of 26 September 1995 (Law 16.719), which substituted Article 280 of the CC, the age until which parents had to respond for their children's wrongdoing was 21. After this law, it was reduced to 18 years. This was much criticized due to the fact that this age is the age at which children commit more wrongdoings (especially, regarding car accidents).

285. It was also criticized because, in Uruguay, parents must pay alimony to their children in some cases until they turn 21 years. This applies in cases children continue studying and cannot earn their own salary. Therefore, these people, who turn 18 years but are clearly insolvent, will not be guaranteed their parent's patrimony in order to compensate for the harm they might cause.

286. The CC not only requires that children be under parental custody but also that they live with them. Notwithstanding this, the authors understand that if parents are absent due to a trip at the time the wrongdoing was committed, they will respond anyway. This requirement will be considered valid also in case, for reasons of studies or sports, the child is provisionally not living with their parents at the time of the wrongdoing. Therefore, for the parents to be free from this liability, they and their child must have been living apart for a long time.

287. The Second Court of Appeal, in a ruling dated 20 May 1991, established that the Civil Codes expression 'live with them' 'does not mean continuous "cohabitation" under the same roof, it suffices that there is a fluid and permanent relationship, that allows the parent with whom the child does not live, to control all the aspects of his child. This duty/right only stops when the child is put in a school, or under the supervision of a teacher or artisan for the learning of an occupation.

(Article 1324, numeral 4)', 'to maintain a strict criterion of the cohabitation, in some hypothesis, would authorize to set free from liability the parent that has avoided the child's custody, and that at the same time could be the cause of why the child committed the wrongdoing, due to the moral abandonment suffered'.[77]

288. Finally, numeral 6 of Article 1324 allows parents to liberate from the presumption of guilt by proving that they acted with the diligence of a good father of the family, in order to avoid the damage (this is a proof of the absence of guilt).

§2. Teachers Liability

289. As was already pointed out, Article 1320 of the CC establishes that 'Neither minors under 10 years, nor mentally impaired are capable of committing a crime or quasi-crime; but the people that are responsible to look after them will be responsible, if they acted with negligence.'

290. Authors had understood that this article, among others, comprises teachers who were taking care of minors under 10 years of age when these minors committed a wrongdoing. In this case, teachers will have to compensate for this damage if the victim proves the damage was caused due to their negligence.

291. Notwithstanding this, Article 1324 of the CC states that school directors are responsible for the damage caused by their students during the time they are under their watch and that this liability will cease when the people mentioned above prove that they employed all of the diligence of a good family father, in order to avoid the damage.

292. Now again, it is very unlikely that a school director will be the one taking care of the school students. Probably, they will be under the watch of the school teacher. Regarding this issue, Professor Gamarra points out that the teacher's liability, when a student causes harm, is determined by the application of Article 1319 of the CC, which states that 'Every unlawful act of men that causes harm to another imposes to the individual whose wilful misconduct, fault or negligence has generated the harm, the duty to repair it (…).'

293. But the director of a school will have to answer, also, due to the fact that in Uruguay, the director is the one in charge of establishing the security measures of the school, controlling the teachers and other employees (which normally do not have the economic situation to repair a damage) and can also hire insurance to cover

77. LJU, 104, 12.026, cited by Jorge Gamarra, in 'Tratado de Derecho Civil Uruguayo', Tomo XX, *supra*, p. 372.

this type of situations.[78] This liability will apply from the moment in which the students enter the school until the moment they leave.[79]

294. Authors had understood that this type of liability comprises situations in which the students are in recess or, even, an outing with teachers.[80] This liability refers only to the directors of schools; therefore, the directors of other establishments which have as a finality to entertain children, but not to educate them, will not be liable (as for example, a day care centre or a summer camp).[81]

§3. Instructors Liability

295. Article 1324 of the CC states that artisans are responsible for the damage caused by their apprentices, during the time they are under their watch, and that this liability will cease when the people mentioned above prove that they employed all of the diligence of a good family father in order to avoid the damage.

296. Therefore, this article states the liability of a person who teaches others art or occupation (such as the art of a carpenter, electrician or plumber). Therefore, only the instructors related to art or occupation will be comprised in the responsibility detailed in this article.

297. Other instructors (i.e., instructors of sports, like waterskiing) will be liable in application of Article 1319 of the CC, which states that 'Every unlawful act of men that causes harm to another imposes to the individual whose wilful misconduct, fault or negligence has generated the harm, the duty to repair it (…).'

298. But the presumption of guilt, determined by Article 1324, will only apply to the instructors of art or occupation. These instructors will be liable during the time they are teaching their apprentices. Authors, such as Professor Gamarra (the most important Uruguayan author of Civil law), state that this type of strict liability, as well as the one stated for the school directors and for the guardians, is excessive and, for this reason, should be revoked.

78. Gamarra, *ibid.*, p. 399.
79. Le Tourneaou, n. 1664, p. 588, Viney, n. 899, p. 994, cited by Gamarra, 'Tratado de Derecho Civil Uruguayo', Tomo XX, *supra*, p. 397.
80. Mazeud, n. 810, p. 745, Alessandri Rodríguez, n. 268, 355, cited by Gamarra, 'Tratado de Derecho Civil Uruguayo', Tomo XX, *supra*, p. 397.
81. Gamarra, 'Tratado de Derecho Civil Uruguayo', Tomo XX, *supra*, p. 397.

Chapter 3. Liability for Things and Animals

§1. Liability for Things

299. According to Article 1324 of the CC:

> There is a duty to repair, not only the damage caused by one's own acts, but also the one caused by an act of the people that a person has under his dependence, or by the things of which a person serves, or that are under his care (…) This liability will cease, when the people mentioned above proof that they employed all of the diligence of a good family father, in order to avoid the damage.

300. Therefore, according to this article, a person is liable for the things he has under his care. In Uruguayan law, animals are equivalent to things. After stating this, Article 1327 of the CC establishes that:

> The owner of a building is liable for the damage that its wreckage causes, if it is due to the omission of the necessary repairs, or due to the lacking in other way, of the due care that a good father of family would have had. If the wreckage came from a defect of construction, the victim can only repeat against the architect that directed the construction of the building, according to what establishes Chapter II, Title IV, Second Part of this Book (Article 1844).

301. Article 1844 was already analysed, in its original version and in its new version (which applies for contracts signed from 13 January 2019 onwards), in numeral 167.

302. Finally, Article 1330 of the CC states that:

> the damage caused by a thing that falls or is thrown from the superior part of a building is attributable to all of the people that live in that part of the building, and the compensation will be divided among all of them, unless it is proven that the damage was caused due to the fault or malice of only one person, in which case this person will be the only one liable.

303. According to Professor Peirano, some time ago, liability for things was explained in the theory of the presumed guilt, which states that in cases in which a thing causes harm, there is a presumption of guilt and, therefore, the victim only has to prove the harm suffered, and after this, the defendant will have to demonstrate that he acted with the diligence of a good father of the family.

304. Afterwards, Besson[82] and Mazeud[83] explained this liability in the system of proven guilt or guilt in the guardianship. These theories imply that the guardian of a thing has the legal obligation to guard it, which configures an obligation of result.

305. Also, it is important to point out that, in Uruguayan law, there are two types of guard: material guard (when the person is in contact with the thing) and legal guard (when the person has a legal right over the thing). In the case of liability for things, the Civil Code establishes the liability of the guardian even in the case where he loses contact with the thing (material guard). Following this, other theories, such as the theory of risk and the theory of warranty, tried to explain the liability for things. Currently, the predominant theory to explain this liability is the theory of guilt (and not a case of strict liability).

306. Regarding jurisprudence, we deem convenient to comment on the ruling, 101/2014, of 25 June 2014, in which the victim sued a company that rented cars, arguing that a foreigner, in a car accident, caused them injuries and that the car he was driving was the property of the defendant's company.

307. The District Court ruled in favour of the defendant because it understood that the defendant could not be sued because he did not cause the accident. The Appellate Court, in its ruling, confirmed the District Court's sentence for the following reasons: 'The plaintiffs argued that, in application of Article 1324 of the CC, the rental company had to compensate the damages caused to the plaintiffs.'

308. The court pointed out that Article 1324 states the legal duty to compensate the damage caused by the things 'that one uses, or that are under his care'. It states that, according to Professor Gamarra, a guardian is he who exercises an effective and independent power of use, direction and control over the thing[84] at the time of the wrongdoing. Also, according to Gamarra, liability, in this case, is not a strict liability but is found in the guilt.

309. Notwithstanding this, other important Uruguayan civil authors, such as Professors Beatriz Venturini and Dora Szafir (a position that was shared by one of the judges of the Appellate Court who disagreed with the final ruling), understand that it is possible for a person to delegate the care of a thing in another, without using it. This way, the person, in some way, uses the thing and benefits from this

82. Besson, 'La notion de garde (tesis)', Paris, 1927, cited by Jorge Peirano, 'Responsabilidad Extracontractual', Editorial Barreiro y Ramos S.A., Montevideo, 1954.
83. Mazeud, La faute dans la garde, publicado en la Revue Trimestrielle de Droit Civil, año 1925, pág. 793 y ss, and then in his Traité théorique et pratique de la responsabilité civile délictuelle et contractuelle, Paris, 1938, to. 2, pag. 304, N° 1312 y ss.
84. Jorge Gamarra, 'Tratado de Derecho Civil Uruguayo', Tomo XXI, 3ª.ed., 2004, Montevideo, pp. 153–159.

use even though he does not have the material guard of the thing. Therefore, he would be liable, in application of the theory of risk and of guilt.[85]

310. Nevertheless, the Appellate Court, in application of the thesis of Professor Gamarra, understood that the owner will only be liable as a guardian of the thing that caused damages, when he has the use and care of it, and even though there will be a presumption that he was the one using it at the time of the wrongdoing, this presumption will be destroyed when it is proven that he transferred the material guard to someone else who was using it at the time of the accident. The court points out that the one who had to be sued in this proceeding was the insurance company and not the car rental company.

311. Regarding the case of car rental companies, we deem it important to point out that this has been discussed profusely by Civil law authors. For example, Dr Van Rompaey, when he was a Supreme Court Minister, disagreed with a ruling stating that to declare the car rental companies not guilty whenever a client of it has an accident produces unfair rulings, which leaves the victim defenceless, and benefits the insurance companies, which will never have to cover the damages caused by an accident in these cases.[86]

312. Also, Professors Carnelli[87] and Mello[88] state that to understand this matter, it is important to focus not only in the relationship between the victim and the car guardian but also other important aspects should be considered, such as the relationship between the company and the car driver and that between the company and the insurance company, due to the fact that the law establishes the duty of the company to hire a damage insurance.

313. According to Carnelli, the company is obliged by law to hire insurance because, afterwards, this insurance, in case of an accident, must cover the damages caused by the car renter. Indeed, the law expressly states that the insurance company will have to cover such damages, 'notwithstanding who had the material guard of the car at the time of the accident or loss'. Therefore, the insurance company, when renting the car, collects from the renter the price of the insurance premium and, therefore, the renter should have the possibility to ask for the insurance coverage in case of a loss or accident.

314. Dr Mello, regarding this issue, states that the victim has a direct action against the insurance company not only to collect the amount of the mandatory insurance but also to collect the total amount of the coverage if the damages rise to

85. Beatriz Venturini & Dora Szafir, 'Legitimados pasivos en la responsabilidad contractual por hecho de las cosas. Nueva lectura del art.1324 inc.1 del Código Civil' en A.D.C.U. Tomo XXIV, pp. 625–629.
86. S.C.J. sentencia N°84 de 19/7/06, published in A.D.C.U. Tomo XXXVII p. 739/743.
87. Carnelli, Santiago, 'Reparación de los daños causados a terceros por conductores arrendatarios de vehículos de alquiler', published in A.D.C.U. Tomo XXXVII, pp 748–760.
88. José Mello ('Acción directa del tercero damnificado contra el asegurador del arrendador de vehículos sin chofer' en A.D.C.U. Tomo XXXIX, pp. 854–867).

this or above this quantity (this article was written after Law No. 18.412 was enacted, which establishes the obligation to hire an Automobile Mandatory Insurance (SOA).

§2. LIABILITY FOR ANIMALS

315. Article 1328 of the CC states that:

> the owner of an animal is liable for the damage that causes, even after becoming free or lost, unless its freedom, loss or damage cannot be attributed to the guilt of the owner, or of his dependents in charge of taking care of the animal. What is established for the owner, is applicable to every person that uses someone else's animal, notwithstanding his action against the owner, if the damage came from a defect of the animal, that the owner must have known and warn and that the owner did not inform about.

316. Regarding this, we deem it important to point out a case in which a person sued after being attacked by three dogs. In this case, the Fourth Civil Appellate Court, in ruling 197/2013 dated 6 November 2013, established that:

> VII) The Court has repeatedly established that, in cases of liability for damage caused by non-ferocious animals, as in this case, Article 1328 C.C. must apply, which reaffirms the general rules of liability for damage caused by things, established in Article 1324 (which also can be used to fulfil the loopholes of this regulation), consolidating an hypothesis of liability of a subjective nature, that determines the establishment of a presumption of guilt –causation 'iuris-tantum', that can be surpassed (totally or partially) if it is proven, (…) the absence of guilt or a strange cause.[89] And, regarding Article 1324 C.C., this regulation does not individualize the person liable for the wrongdoing, but it attributes responsibility to the guardian, who is defined as the person that has an effective and independent power of use, direction and control, over the thing that causes the damage, who is normally the owner of the thing; recognizing that the presumption of guard that levies on the owner can be surpassed when it is proven, (…) that this control was transferred without guilt.[90]

317. Therefore, according to the main civil authors of Uruguay and the Uruguayan jurisprudence, in the case of liability for the damage caused by non-wild or fierce animals, this damage will be attributed to the owner of the animal, who, in order to be liberated from responsibility, must prove that: (i) he acted without guilt or that the damage was caused due to a strange cause, or (ii) that the control of the animal, before the damage was caused, was transferred to another person (who would be the one liable for the damage caused).

89. Gamarra, 'Tratado de Derecho Civil', Tomo XIX, *supra*, p. 339.
90. *Ibid.*, p. 249.

318. Now, regarding fierce animals, Article 1329 of the CC, establishes that:

> the damage caused by a wild or fierce animal, will always be attributable to whom has it under his care, notwithstanding if this person is his owner or not, and even if it was not possible for him to avoid the wrongdoing, and even if the animal had released itself without his fault.

319. The aforesaid will not be applicable to the authorities and public servants of the parks or State or municipal zoos to whom what was established in the precedent article will apply (in Article 1328, analysed in numeral 315). The same rule will apply to the owners of private parks or zoos, their guardians and dependents in charge of watching the animals.

320. Regarding this article, Uruguayan jurisprudence has understood the following, in the ruling 71/2005 dated on 13 April 2005, and issued by the First Civil Appellate Court (in a case where a bull caused a car accident):

> VIII. In case of admitting, that the defendant liability is regulated by Article 1329 of the Civil Code, due to the fact that the damage was caused by a wild or fierce animal (a bull), which obliges he who owned the animal, to compensate the harm caused by it, even if it was not possible to prevent the harm, and even if the animal would have had set free without the guilt of their guardians, then the obligation to compensate would configure independently from the behaviour of the direct or indirect agent of the damage.[91]

321. Therefore, in this case, unlike the precedent article and due to the wildness or fierceness of the animal, its owner will have to compensate for the damage it causes, without regard of his acting with diligence.

322. Finally, Article 1329.1 of the Civil Uruguayan Code states that:

> Regarding the precedent article, it will be considered a fierce or wild animal those who are not usually tamable, or which are dangerous for human beings, due to its aggressiveness, costumes, size or strength, such as big felines, pachyderms, bears, crocodiles, poisonous reptiles, boa constrictor, big and medium primates, wolfs, jungle cats, wild boars and similar.

323. 'This qualification is not excluded by the fact that the animal has been raised by human beings and in a domestic regime.'

324. This way, Article 1329.1 defines a fierce or wild animal but leaves room ('and similar') for the judges to understand, in a case-by-case basis, if they are before this type of animal and, therefore, Article 1329 must be applied.

---

91. Conf. Ordoqui-Olivera 'Derecho Extracontractual' Vol. II, pp. 245/247.

Part III. Forms of Strict Liability

Chapter 1. Road and Traffic Accidents

325. In the case of traffic accidents, it has been said that it is fair that the person creating the risk be the one that suffers its consequences. This is why Professor Gamarra, in his treaty, proposes, in 2000, the enactment of a mandatory car insurance, in order that, in case of an accident, the insurance company pays the victim – without mattering if the driver was responsible for the accident – a compensation for the damage caused.[92]

326. This suggestion (with some delay) was heard by legislators and, on 19 August 2009, when all of Europe and various countries of other continents had already enacted this type of law, the SOA Law No. 18.412 was enacted. The decree that regulates this law is the Decree No. 381/009.

327. This law establishes that all self-propelled vehicles and trailers must have this insurance. The law also includes motorcycles, but it first established that it was mandatory for motorcycles, except for those with an inferior capacity than 70 cc, that had been registered before 19 August 2009 (which would have to hire this insurance, but had a longer period to do it).

328. This insurance covers only those personal injuries or death, caused by the insured car to a third party, in an accident. It does not cover material damages.

329. In the case of the automobiles that were already insured, their owners did not have to hire a new insurance. It was enough that the insurance policy already hired had the minimum coverage established by the SOA.

330. It is mandatory to drive with a sticker that says SOA, which has to be placed on the windshield or other easily visible place. This law forbids the circulation of vehicles that do not have this insurance (Article 1).

331. The automobiles that are excluded from this law are the following: those that circulate on rails, those that are used exclusively in places where the public does not have access, those that are placed into an impoundment lot and, in general, those that are not used for traffic circulation (Article 3).

---

92. Gamarra, 'Tratado de Derecho Civil Uruguayo', Tomo XIX, *supra*, p. 60.

332. The vehicles that are registered abroad, or that enter the country in a temporary admission regime, are also obliged to have SOA, notwithstanding the international agreements celebrated between Uruguay and other States (Article 4).

333. This law does not consider third parties (and therefore, will not be covered by the SOA):

(A) The owner of the vehicle, the insurance holder and the driver, as well as the spouse or domestic partner, ancestors, descendants (of the same bloodline or not, or due to adoption), and the collateral relatives until the second grade), regarding the insurance of the same vehicle.
(B) Dependents of the owner, of the insurance holder or of the driver, when they are in the same vehicle, or performing tasks under other insurance coverage.
(C) The people transported in the vehicle for valuable consideration who have other insurance coverage.
(D) The occupants of stolen vehicles, unless they prove they did not know of this circumstance, or that they were there against their will.
(E) The victim or his beneficiaries, when the victim acted with malice, in the causation of his injuries or death.

334. The insurance holder will be the owner of the vehicle, its user or he who has the material guard of the vehicle (i.e., who is in possession of it at the moment) (Article 7).

335. The maximum coverage of this insurance is of UI (Indexed Unit) 250,000 (currently, 1 UI = UYU 5,1465), which would amount to approximately USD 29,241, for each vehicle and for each accident.

336. The injuries will be compensated according to a percentage of the total amount of coverage. The total and permanent incapacity might rise to 100% of the coverage (Article 8). If there is more than one injured party, then the compensation will adjust proportionally to the amount insured without being possible to exceed this amount (Article 9).

337. The payment of compensations in reference to a policy will not imply the reduction of the amount covered and will not modify the premium paid (Article 9). The insurance companies must inform the Insurance and Reinsurance Superintendence (SSR) about the conditions and premiums that they will apply regarding each category of vehicles (Article 11).

338. The insurance companies authorized to provide car insurance must operate with the SOA and cannot refuse to provide coverage unless the vehicle does not gather all the insurance conditions established by the SSR (Article 11).

339. In case an accident has happened, the victim or his beneficiaries must file a claim directly before the insurance company, proving his right and the damage suffered and submitting all the proof elements they have (Article 12).

340. After receiving the claim, the insurance company will answer the claimant(s) within a period that cannot exceed thirty working days (Article 12). If the company, after this period, does not answer the claimants, they can file a lawsuit (Article 12).

341. The statute of limitations established by this law is of two years, which starts from the moment of the accident that caused the damage. This period will be interrupted by the causes established by law (Article 14).

342. The insurer cannot raise, against the victim and his beneficiaries, a defence that it has regarding the insured. Neither can it raise a defence of an act of God or of force majeure or allege the act of a third party (Article 15).

343. After paying the compensations, the insurance companies can claim these payments to the owner of the vehicle, or the insurance holder, in the following cases: (i) in case of breach of contract; (ii) when the vehicle did not have an insurance in force; (iii) when the damage was caused due to the act of malice of the owner, user or driver or due to a gross fault in the maintenance of the vehicle; or (iv) when the destination of the vehicle was changed, increasing significantly the risk of an accident.

344. If the accident is generated by an unidentified vehicle, one that does not have SOA, or a vehicle which was stolen, the injured or his beneficiaries will be compensated through a special proceeding (Articles 19–22).

345. In these cases, the compensation will be paid by the Special Coverage Compensation Fund, which will be administered by the National Unit of Road Security (UNASEV) (Articles 19–22).

346. If the vehicle comprised in this law is already insured by an insurance that covers civil liability of the insured in a higher amount than the one established in the SOA, then this vehicle will have complied with the law (there's no need to purchase a new insurance) (Article 23).

347. The right of the victims and their beneficiaries, according to this law, does not affect the one they might have for a higher compensation, according to other laws. The compensations paid due to SOA coverage will be deducted from the amounts the defendant must pay for a higher amount if it refers to the same damages (Article 24).

348. The Ministry of Interior and the Municipalities will be in charge of controlling the compliance with this law. In case of road accidents with injured parties, the control of the Ministry of Interior will be mandatory (Article 26).

349. Without the previous control of the SOA in force, (i) the Public Registries will not be able to register car property titles, pledge contracts or other documents that affect the ownership of the vehicles (Article 27); (ii) the Municipalities will not be able to perform transfers, registrations, changes of motor or chassis, give certificates of free of debt and records (Article 27).

350. These offices must verify that the vehicles have been insured with the SOA since the law is in force. In case they did not, the vehicle owners will have to pay a fine equivalent to the average amount of the cost of this insurance in the market (Article 28).

351. The vehicles owned by the Uruguayan State are comprised in this law (Article 29). The regulations of this law are of public order (and, therefore, parties cannot agree with them) (Article 30). This law has been in force since 19 August 2009.

Chapter 2. Product Liability

352. Product liability in Uruguay was regulated by the CC, until 11 August 2000, when the Act 17.250 was enacted on 11 August 2000. After the enactment of this law, Decree No. 308/002 (abrogated on 9 August 2002), Decree No. 16/004 of 21 January 2004 and Decree No. 503/006 of 4 December 2006 were enacted in order to regulate Law 17.250.

353. Law 17.250 is of public order and, therefore, parties cannot agree against it (Article 1). In this law, it is stated that when a situation is not foreseen by it, the Uruguayan Code will apply.

354. In Uruguay, a consumer is 'any person, or legal entity, that purchases or uses products or services, as a final recipient, in a consumption relationship, or based on it. It is not considered a consumer or user he who, without being a final recipient, acquires, stocks up, uses or consumes products or services, in order to integrate them to his production, transformation or trade process' (Article 2).

355. While a supplier is defined as 'any person, or legal entity, national or foreign, private or public, and in the latter, governmental or non-governmental, that carries out in a professional manner, the production, creation, construction, transformation, assembly, import, distribution and commerce, of products or services, within a consumption relationship' (Article 3).

356. A consumption relationship in Uruguay occurs when there is a bond between the supplier who, for a valuable consideration, delivers a product or provides a service to a final recipient (Article 4).

357. Notwithstanding the requirement of a valuable consideration, 'the delivery of products and the provision of services which are made free of charge, will be considered consumption relationships when they are performed depending upon a possible consumption relationship'.

358. Product is defined as any corporeal or incorporeal thing, movable or immovable, while service is defined as any remunerated activity, provided in the consumer market, except those which take place in labour relationships (Article 5).

§1. Basic Rights of a Consumer

359. In Uruguay, the basic rights of the consumer are the following (Article 6):

(i) Protection to his life, health and security from risks caused by the practices in the provision of goods and services considered dangerous or damaging.
(ii) The education and publicity regarding the adequate use of the products and services, the freedom to choose and the egalitarian treatment at the moment of the celebration of the contract.

(iii) Provision of sufficient information, which has to be clear, truthful, and in Spanish, notwithstanding other languages that can be used in addition.
(iv) Protection from deceitful publicity, coercive or disloyal methods, in the provision of products or services, and abusive clauses in contracts of adhesion, each of them within the terms of Law 17.250.
(v) The association in organizations whose specific object is the consumer defence and to be represented by them.
(vi) The effective prevention and compensation of the patrimonial and extra-patrimonial damages. The access to judicial and administrative organisms for the prevention and compensation of the harm caused, through agile and efficient proceedings, in the terms established by Law 17.250.

360. Regarding the situation in which the supplier of a product or service, after introducing it to the market, becomes aware of its dangerousness, Article 11 states his obligation to communicate these situations immediately to the authorities and to consumers through public announcements.

§2. Offer and Acceptance

361. Regarding matters such as offer and acceptance, Article 12 of Law 17.250 has a different position from the one established by the CC. Indeed, this article states that an offer addressed to determinate or indeterminate consumers, transmitted by any means of communication, that includes sufficient and precise information regarding products or services offered, will bind he who makes the offer and he who accepts it expressly, during the time the offer is made.

362. This is different from what the Civil Code stipulates due to the fact that, according to the Civil Code, an offer has to be directed to determinate persons. Therefore, if the offer is directed to indeterminate persons, this offer will constitute an invitation to offering and not an offer, strictly speaking.

363. The period of time of the offer will be extended in the following cases:

(1) When this offer is issued on a non-working day, in which case this offer will bind the parties until the first working day after the offer was made.
(2) When the one making the offer establishes a longer period.

In all cases, the offer can specify its modalities, conditions or limitations.

364. During the period of validity of the offer, and even if this period is longer than the one provided by law, the offer can be revoked. Revocation will be effective once it is disseminated by similar means to the ones used to communicate it and as long as this happens before the acceptance arrives at the offeror. Notwithstanding this, if the offeror assumes the commitment to not revoke the offer, then it will not be revocable.

365. The acceptance of the offer must be in a timely fashion. If not, it will not be effective, unless the offeror decides to grant effectiveness to it. If an offer gave contradictory information, the one which is more favourable to the consumer will prevail.

366. Finally, all information, even the one published in advertising, disseminated by any means, binds the offeror who ordered its broadcasting and any other person who uses it and becomes part of the contract celebrated with the consumer (Article 14).

367. The supplier shall inform, in all the offers made previously to the formalization of the contract, among others, the total price of the product or service offered (taxes included).

368. If an offer for the provision of products or services is made outside the company's commercial establishment (by mail, telephone, television, email, etc.), then according to Article 16 of the law, the consumer will have the right to rescind this contract *ipso jure* (by the mere operation of law). The consumer will be able to exercise this right within five working days from the day of the formalization of the contract or from the delivery of the product, without any responsibility for him. This option must be communicated to the supplier by any reliable means of communication. Also, when the offer of services is made in a place set up to offer, the consumer will also have this right.

369. If the consumer exercised this right, he will have to give back the product to the supplier, without having used it, in the same state in which it was received, except for the changes caused to confirm its good condition. After receiving it, the supplier must give back to the consumer the purchase price. If it was paid with a credit card, it will suffice that the consumer informs the issuers of these cards about the option made.

370. In case of services partially provided, the consumer will pay only for the part that was provided, and if the service was prepaid, then the supplier must immediately give back the amount referred to the part of the service that was not provided. The supplier must inform the consumer, in writing, in the contract, in a clear and understandable way, about the right of the consumer to terminate the contract. If the supplier does not comply with this duty, the consumer can exercise this right at any moment.

371. The offer of products must furnish clear and legible information about its characteristics, nature, quantity, quality, composition, warranty, origin, price, conservation and use of the product, validity period and risks it might have for the health and security of the consumer (Article 17).

372. Manufacturers and importers of products should ensure the offer of components and replacements while the manufacture or import of the said products continues (Article 18). The offer of defective, used or restored products must indicate this circumstance in a clear and visible way.

373. The information must be clear and truthful, and when the offer is in writing, it must be provided in an easily readable font. In the offer of services, the supplier must inform about the following, unless due to the nature of the service, it does not correspond:

(a) Name and domicile of the supplier of the service.
(b) Description of the service to be provided.
(c) A description of the materials, utensils, technology to be used, and the period or periods during which the service will be provided.
(d) The price, taxes and the way of payment.
(e) The risks that the service might generate for the health or security of the consumer.
(f) The scope and duration of the warranty, when it is provided (Article 20).

§3. Abusive Practices in the Offer

374. According to Article 22 of Law 17.250, the following are considered abusive practices in the offer:

(a) To deny the provision of products or services to a consumer during a time in which it is possible to provide them, except when the offer has been limited and this has been informed to the consumer.
(b) To broadcast information that discredits the consumer, due to the actions carried out by him in the exercise of his rights.
(c) To establish the period, or periods, for the compliance of obligations, in a disproportionate way, to the detriment of the consumer.
(d) To send or deliver to the consumer, any product or to provide any service that was not previously requested. The services provided and the products delivered to the consumer, in this hypothesis, will not entail an obligation to pay them, or give them back, and shall be received as free samples.
(e) To make the consumer appear as the one asking for the acquisition of goods or services.
(f) To condition the provision of products or services, to the provision of other products or services, as well as to condition them to quantitative limits, without a just cause.

§4. Contractual Warranty of Products and Services

375. The supplier of products and services that offers a warranty shall offer it in writing, and it must be standardized for identical products (Article 23 of Law

17.250). This warranty must be easily understandable and legible and must inform the consumer about the scope of its most significant aspects.

376. It must contain at least the following information:

(a) Identification of the person offering the warranty.
(b) Identification of the manufacturer or importer of the product or supplier of the service.
(c) Precise identification of the product or service, with the basic technical specifications.
(d) Warranty validity conditions, its duration and coverage, specifying the parts of the product or service covered by it.
(e) Domicile and phone information of those who are contractually obliged to provide it.
(f) Conditions for the reparation of the product or service, with the specification of the place where the warranty will be made effective.
(g) Costs to be paid by the consumer, if any.
(h) Place and date in which the product will be delivered or the service will be provided.

377. The warranty certificate must be completed by the supplier and delivered along with the product or at the end of the provision of the service. If the certificate is delivered by the businessman but in it the manufacturer or importer is identified as the one offering the warranty, the latter will be the one bounded by the accessory warranty contract.

§5. Advertising

378. Advertising must be transmitted and broadcasted in a way in which the consumer can identify it as advertising (Article 24 of Law 17.250). Deceitful advertising is prohibited. The law defines deceitful advertising as any modality of information or communication included in advertising messages, which is totally or partially false, or in any way, even by the omission of essential information, is capable of leading the consumer to a mistake regarding the nature, quantity, origin or price of the products or services offered.

379. Comparative advertising is allowed by Law 17.250 (Article 25) as long as it is based on the objectivity of the comparison and not on subjective data of a psychological or emotional nature; and as long as the comparison can be subject to verification. The burden of proof of the truthfulness and material accuracy of the factual information included in the information or communication advertised will belong to the advertiser (Article 26). If a company understands that a competitor is being deceitful through its advertising, it can file a complaint before the Self-regulation of Advertising National Council (Consejo Nacional de Autoregulación Publicitaria – CONARP), which has the power to sanction this type of behaviour.

§6. Adhesion Contract

380. The adhesion contract is defined by law as the contract in which the clauses or conditions have been established unilaterally by the supplier of products or services, without allowing the consumer to discuss, negotiate or modify substantially its content. In the written contracts, the inclusion of additional clauses to the ones established in advance does not change the nature of the contract (Article 28).

381. The adhesion contracts will be written in Spanish, in clear terms and in an easily legible font, so that this facilitates the understanding of the consumer (Article 29).

§7. Abusive Clauses in the Adhesion Contracts

382. A clause will be abusive, in its content or in its form, when it establishes clear and unjustified imbalances between the rights and duties of the contracting parties, in detriment to the consumers, as well as any clause that violates the duty to act in good faith. The appraisal of the abusive nature of the clauses will not refer to the product or service or to the price or compensation of the contract, as long as these clauses are written in a clear and comprehensive way (Article 30).

383. The following, among others, are considered abusive clauses (Article 31):

(a) Clauses that exonerate or limit the liability of the supplier for defects of any nature, of the products or services, unless a regulation allows it or unless another cause justifies it.
(b) The clauses that imply that the consumer waives rights.
(c) The clauses that authorize the supplier to modify the terms of the contract.
(d) The resolutory clause agreed exclusively in favour of the supplier. Its inclusion does not deprive the consumer from asking for the compliance of the contract.
(e) The clauses that contain any precept that imposes the burden of proof to the detriment of the consumer, when legally it does not correspond.
(f) Clauses that impose representatives to the consumer.
(g) Clauses that imply that the consumer waives his right to be compensated or reimbursed from any expenditure that legally corresponds to the supplier.
(h) Clauses that establish that the silence of the consumers will be understood as acceptance, of any modification, restraint or expansion of what was agreed in the contract.
(i) Clauses that establish the automatic renewal of the contract, not allowing the consumer to disengage from the contract without liability. The consumer will be able to rescind or resolve the contract within sixty consecutive days, counted from the date in which the automatic renewal took place, communicating this to the supplier with a prior notice of fifteen continuous days.

384. The inclusion of abusive clauses gives the right to the consumer to demand the nullity of them, and in this case the judge will integrate the contract. If, after doing so, the judge understands that with the integrated content of the contract, the contract lacks cause, he can declare the nullity of the contract (Article 31, modified by Law 19.149).

§8. BREACH

385. The infringement of the supplier of the duty to act with good faith or the violation of the duty to inform in the pre-contractual stage or in the stage of celebration, or in the one of execution of the contract, will give the right to the consumer to opt between reparation, resolution or compliance with the contract. In all cases, the consumer will have the right to ask also for the compensatory damages that correspond.

386. The breach of the supplier, to any of his obligations, unless a non-imputable cause justified it, allows the consumer to (Article 33):

(a) Demand the forced compliance of the obligation, as long as this is possible.
(b) Accept other products or services, or compensation.
(c) Solve the contract, and demand the devolution of what was paid, updated, or rescind the contract, depending on what corresponds.

387. In any of these options, the consumer will have the right to the compensation of the compensatory and penalty damages suffered, depending on what corresponds.

§9. LIABILITY FOR DAMAGES (ARTICLE 34)

388. If the defect or risk of the product or service causes harm to the consumer, the supplier will be responsible according to the regime established in the Civil Code. The businessman or distributor will only be liable when the importer and manufacturer cannot be identified. The businessman or distributor will also be liable if the damage is caused as a consequence of an inadequate conservation of the product or when they alter their original conditions.

389. The liability of the professionals will be a strict liability or subjective liability, depending on the nature of the service agreed (Article 35). The supplier will not respond for damages, other than those which are an immediate and direct consequence of the unlawful act, and the damages will include the patrimonial and extra-patrimonial damages (Article 36).

§10. STATUTE OF LIMITATIONS

390. This is referred to in part IV of Chapter 1 of this monograph.

§11. Infractions

391. Infractions regarding matters referred to the defence of consumers will be punished by the General Commerce Office (Dirección General de Comercio) (Article 44). This Office can delegate its power to impose penalties in the Consumer Defence Office (*Dirección del Area de Defensa del Consumidor*).

392. Infractions can be qualified as minor, serious and very serious, attending to the following criteria (Article 46 of the Law): the risk of the health of the consumer, the position of the supplier in the market, the amount of the obtained benefit, the intention, the seriousness of the social alteration produced, the increase on the commission of the infraction and the relapse.

393. After verifying the commission of an infraction and without prejudice of the civil and criminal liability of the wrongdoer, he will be subject to the following sanctions, which can be applied independently or jointly, according to the circumstances (Article 47):

(1) Warning, when the infractor does not have any records in the commission of infractions of the same nature and when this infraction is qualified as minor.
(2) Fine, which amount will not be inferior to UR 20 (currently, USD 620), and can amount to UR 4,000 (currently, USD 124,030).
(3) Confiscation of the merchandise and products subject to the infraction, when they can entail a clear risk for the health or security of the consumer.
(4) In case of relapse of serious infractions, or in case of a very serious infraction, the authority can order the temporary close down of the supplier's commercial or industrial establishment for up to ninety days.
(5) Suspension up to one year in the registry of suppliers that allows persons and companies to hire with the State.

394. Also, when serious infractions are verified, the Defence Consumer Office can put a sign, in the front and the interior of the establishment, in which it is pointed out that the supplier is an infractor to the Consumer Protection Act. This can last up to twenty days, from the date of the verification of the infraction.

395. In case of relapses in similar infractions, when the intent of the infraction is proven or if there are circumstances that entail a risk for the health or safety of the consumers, the authority can order a publication, in newspapers of national diffusion, of the decision to sanction the supplier, which will be paid by the infractor.

Chapter 3. Liability for Services

396. When the services were rendered to a final consumer, the applicable regimen will be the one referred to in Chapter 2 of part III, along with product liability (Act 17.250).

397. In the remaining cases, and in case of the Consumer Protection Act (Law 17.250) does not regulate the situation presented in a consumer relationship, the Civil Code will apply. The rendering of services is regulated in the CC, in Article 1831, which states that: 'A contract for the rendering of services will exist when one of the parties agrees to render a service, and the other agrees to pay her a pecuniary price for this service.'

398. Article 1832 of the CC states that if a person agrees to render a service for free, or for a non-pecuniary retribution, this contract will not be understood as a rendering of services but, nevertheless, will be regulated by this chapter, when applicable.

399. The CC, in Article 1833, states that any service or work, material or immaterial, mechanical or white collar, can be subject to this contract. Even though the remuneration of this service or work has the name of fees or rights, the contract will still be of the rendering of services and not of the mandate, if it does not give the power of representation to the person hired. This article expressly includes, as a contract for the rendering of services, those celebrated with lawyers and even advanced law students, when they act without the power of representation of their clients.

400. Article 1834 of the CC states that he who worked for someone else or who rendered a service to another person can sue him for the price of it, even in cases where no payment of a price or retribution was agreed to, as long as this service or work referred to the profession or honest way of living of the person rendering it. In this case, it will be presumed that the parties fixed a custom price which would be determined judicially, in case of doubt. If the service or work rendered, although being honest, was not referred to the profession or way of living of the person doing it, the aforesaid will only apply when, taking into account the circumstances, it could not be inferred that the intention of this person was to benefit the person for whom the work or service was rendered. This intention will be presumed if the service was not requested or if the person who rendered it was living in the house of the party benefited by it.

401. Article 1835 refers to the services rendered by someone in favour of the person who raised him and states that in this case, the latter cannot be forced to pay the salary for the services rendered to the person who was raised by him until he turns 15 years old. This article will also apply to legal guardians when they live with the minors of whom they are in charge of.

402. The Civil Code, in Article 1836, establishes that no one can oblige to render services if not temporarily or for a particular work. This article is very important, especially when referred to distribution contracts and contracts without a due date. In these cases, jurisprudence has understood that any of the parties can finish the contract at any time and without cause, in the application of this article. Nevertheless, jurisprudence has stated that parties must calculate a reasonable notice period for the termination of this contract, which judges have determined, should be between 30 and 180 days, depending on the contract in hand.

403. Articles 1840–1855 of the CC regulate the case of the construction contract. Article 1844 establishes that the architect and the businessman in charge of the construction will be liable for a period of ten years, for the damages caused in case the construction collapses due to a defect in the construction or in the land. This article was modified by Law 19.726 and is commented in point 167.

404. Article 1845 states that when a businessman has obliged to make a construction for a fixed price, he cannot ask, later, for a raise even if the labour cost or the materials cost varies, unless the owner authorizes modifications in the initial proposal.

405. If someone requests a construction for which the worker has to purchase the materials, he can terminate the contract, even though the construction has been started, by compensating the worker of all the expenses and work done and of the lost profits. This article has been commented on a lot in civil doctrine because it is one of the very few cases in which the law allows one of the contracting parties to terminate a contract for a specific work, without a just cause.

406. Article 1854 states that he who has performed work over a movable thing has the right to withhold it until he is paid. This article is also exceptional because, normally, the person in charge of doing a work is not allowed by law to withhold the work done.

407. Finally, Article 1855 establishes that transport businessmen and transport agents who work on land or at sea, transporting people or things, will be regulated by the commercial law.

Chapter 4. Environmental Liability

§1. Laws that Regulate Environmental Liability

408. In Uruguay, the laws that regulate the protection of the environment are the Constitution, Law No. 16.466 and Law No. 17.283.

409. Law No. 16.466 was enacted on 19 January 1994 and, in its Article 4, it established that:

> Notwithstanding the administrative and criminal sanctions that the law determines, he who causes depredation, destruction or contamination of the environment, going against what is established in the articles of this law, will be civilly liable for all the damages caused, and if possible, will have to take the actions in order to amend the harm done.

When the harm caused due to this violation is irreversible, the person that caused it must take the actions in order to reduce or mitigate to the utmost these harms, notwithstanding the administrative, civil or criminal sanctions that might be applicable. This law was regulated by Decree No. 435/994 (now abrogated).

410. The protection of the environment is specially regulated in the Constitution of the Republic of Uruguay as an issue of general interest. Indeed, in Article 47 of the Constitution, it is established that 'People must refrain from any act that causes serious predation, destruction or contamination to the environment. Law will regulate this disposition and can establish sanctions for the transgressors.' Although the Uruguayan Constitution was enacted in 1967, this article was included in the reform of the Constitution in 1996.

411. On 12 December 2000, Law 17.283 was enacted and, until now, this is the principal law that regulates environmental policy and liability. This law was regulated by Decree No. 152/013 and by Decree No. 222/019.

§2. Law 17.283

I. Issues Regarding the Environment that are of General Interest

412. This law starts by pointing out that it is of general interest, according to what was stated in Article 47 of the Constitution of the Republic:

(a) The protection of the environment, the quality of the air, of the water, of the land and of the landscape.
(b) The preservation of the biological diversity, and the shape and structure of the coastline.
(c) The reduction and the adequate management of toxic or dangerous substances and waste, whatever its type.

(d) The prevention, elimination, mitigation and compensation of negative environmental impacts.
(e) The protection of the shared environmental resources and of the ones located outside the zones submitted to national jurisdiction.
(f) The regional and international environmental cooperation and the involvement in the solution of the global environmental problems.
(g) The formulation, instrumentation and implementation of the national environmental policy and of the sustainable development.

413. For the purposes of this law, it is understood that sustainable development is a development that satisfies the necessities of the present without compromising the capacity of the future generations to satisfy their own necessities.

II. Right of the Inhabitants of the Republic to Enjoy a Healthy Environment

414. After pointing this out, this law establishes the right of the inhabitants of the Republic to be protected in the enjoyment of a healthy and balanced environment (Article 2).

III. Duty of the Persons and Legal Entities to Refrain from Causing Environmental Damage

415. Article 3 of this law states that 'the persons and the legal entities, public and private, have the duty to refrain of any act that causes serious depredation, destruction or contamination to the environment (…)'.

416. It also declares that, regarding what was established in Article 47 of the Constitution of the Republic and in this article, it is considered acts that cause serious depredation, destruction or contamination to the environment, those that violate what is established in the present law and in all the other regulations of the matters referred in Article 1. This law, as well, states that any significant loss, decrease or detriment that is caused to the environment should be understood as environmental.

IV. Duty of the State to Promote an Environmental Sustainable Development

417. This law establishes a fundamental duty of the State and of the public entities, in general, to promote a design of environmentally sustainable development, protecting the environment, and, if it was deteriorated, to recover it or demand its recovery (Article 4).

V. Principles of the National Environmental Policy

418. Regarding principles of environmental policy, Article 6 of the law states that the national environmental policy that the Executive Power determines will use as a basis for the following principles:

(a) The distinction of the Republic, in the context of the nations, as a 'Natural Country', from an economic, cultural and social perspective of sustainable development.
(b) The prevention and prevision are guidelines of first importance regarding any others in the environmental management, and when there is danger of a serious or irreversible damage, it will not be possible to allege the lack of total technical or scientific certainty as a reason for not adopting preventive measures.
(c) It is a requirement for the effective integration of the environmental dimension to the economic and social development, the gradual and progressive incorporation of the new requirements, without recognizing, due to this, the consolidation of pre-existing situations.
(d) The protection of the environment is a commitment that affects the society as a whole and, due to this, the people and social entities have the right as well as the duty to participate in this process.
(e) Environmental management must be performed by acknowledging that it affects multiple sectors and, therefore, it is important to integrate and coordinate the public and private sectors involved, ensuring the national reach of the implementation of the environmental policy and the decentralization in the exercise of the commitments of the environmental protection.
(f) The environmental management must have as a basis adequate management of the environmental information, in order to ensure its availability and accessibility for any interested party.
(g) The increase and strengthening of the international cooperation in environmental issues, promoting the elaboration of common environmental guidelines.

419. The principles aforementioned will also serve as an interpretative criterion in order to solve issues that may arise in the application of rules and responsibilities for the protection of the environment and its relationship with other rules and responsibilities.

VI. Instruments for the Environmental Management

420. Article 7 of the law refers to the instruments for the environmental management. Among others, it mentions the following instruments: law, guidelines, programmes, plans and projects for environmental protection, education, training, the establishment of parameters and standards of environmental quality, the affidavits, the environmental impact statements, the authorization proceedings of the environmental authority, audits, environmental certifications, the system of protected natural areas, economic and tax incentives and the administrative sanctions.

421. The coordination of environmental management is an exclusive responsibility of the Executive Power through the Ministry of Housing, Land Demarcation and Environment (Article 8).

VII. Power of the Ministry of Housing, Land Demarcation and Environment

422. In order to ensure the compliance with what is established in the laws and regulations referred to the protection of the environment, Article 14 of the law allows the Ministry of Housing, Land Demarcation and Environment, among others, to establish rules regarding the process for the treatment of the waste and emissions and to demand the establishment of a warranty for the due compliance of the environmental laws.

VIII. Sanctions in Case of Non-compliance

423. In case of non-compliance of the dispositions that regulate the protection of the environment, the Ministry of Housing, Land Demarcation and Environment can impose the following sanctions (which can be imposed separately or jointly): (i) written warning; (ii) public diffusion of the sanctioning decision; (iii) confiscation of the objects or products of the unlawful activity; and (iv) suspension, for a period that can be of up to 180 days, of the registrations, authorizations or permits for the exercise of the activity of the infractor.

IX. Repair of the Harm Done

424. Regarding the repair of the harm done, Article 16 states that when the person responsible for the damage delays or refuses to the repair, reduction or mitigation of the damage caused, he can be punished with fines or he can be obliged to pay for the cost of it.

X. Prohibition to Liberate or Emit Substances Over the Maximum Limits

425. This law also forbids the liberation or emission into the atmosphere, directly or indirectly, of substances, materials or energy over the maximum limits or against the conditions that the Ministry of Housing, Land Demarcation and Environment establishes (Article 17).

XI. Protection of the Ozone Layer

426. Regarding the ozone layer, Article 18 states that the Ministry of Housing, Land Demarcation and Environment, in its capacity of national authority for the purposes of the instrumentation and application of the Vienna Convention for the Protection of the Ozone Layer (1985), as well as for the purposes of the Montreal Protocol on Substances that Deplete the Ozone Layer (1987), can establish the deadlines, limits and restrictions to the production, commerce and use of the substances that affects it.

XII. Climate Change

427. This law also includes an article (Article 19) regarding Climate Change and states that the Ministry of Housing, Land Demarcation and Environment, as the national authority for the purposes of the instrumentation and application of the United Nations Framework Convention on Climate Change (1992), will establish the measures for the mitigation of the causes and the adjustment to the consequences of the climate change and, especially, will regulate the emission of the gases with the greenhouse effect.

XIII. Use and Handling of Chemical Substances

428. Law 17.283 states that it is of general interest the protection of the environment, regarding the use and handling of chemical substances, especially the ones considered toxic or dangerous (Article 20), as well as regarding the handling and disposal of waste (Article 21).

XIV. Biologic Diversity

429. Law 17.283 points out in Article 22 that it is of general interest the preservation and the sustainable use of biological diversity as a fundamental key to the national environmental policy as well as in order to instrument and apply the Convention on Biological Diversity (1992).

XV. Biosafety

430. Regarding biosafety issues, Article 23 states that the Ministry of Housing, Land Demarcation and Environment will establish rules and will apply measures in order to prevent and control the environmental risks derived from the creation, handling, use or release of genetically modified organisms, as a result of biotechnological applications, as long as they can affect the preservation and sustainable use of the biological diversity and the environment.

431. The introduction of living, modified organisms resulting from biotechnology in the zones submitted to national jurisdiction will be subject to the previous authorization of the competent authority.

XVI. Simplified Proceeding for the Collection of Sanctions, and Expenses Derived from Sanctions Imposed Due to the Damage Caused to the Environment

432. Article 28 of Law 17.283 states that the resolutions that establish the expenses derived from the imposition of sanctions due to the violation of rules regarding the protection of the environment, and the resolutions that establish the expenses incurred in the repair, reduction or mitigation of the environmental impact, as well as the resolutions that impose the fines, will constitute an executive title (and therefore, a simplified proceeding will be allowed to collect this amounts). The judges that will be competent to know about the collection of these amounts will be the District Court judges of the domicile of the defendant.

433. This article also states that when the defendant is the Ministry of Housing, Land Demarcation and Environment, the competent judges will be the ones of Montevideo.

§3. Lead Poisoning Cases

434. After reviewing the regulations referred to environment protection, we deem it important to point out that within Uruguay, the principal issue that has been discussed referred to environmental liability is the one regarding lead poisoning.

435. One of the principal rulings regarding this matter was the Ruling no. 158/008 of 16 July 2008, in which the First Civil Appellate Court confirmed the ruling of the Second Contentious Administrative District Court regarding a case of lead poisoning.

436. The District Court, in this ruling, ordered the defendants: the Ministry of Housing, Land Demarcation and Environment and the Municipality of Montevideo, to pay UYU 50,000 (USD 2,203), plus adjustments and interests to the mother of the child poisoned, and UYU 60,000 (USD 2,643) plus adjustments and interests to the child with lead poisoning, for pain and suffering.

437. The defendants appealed and the Appellate Court confirmed this ruling in virtue of the following reasons:

(1) Although in this case, after finding out that the plaintiff (Nicolás Amoroso, a 9-year-old boy) suffered lead poisoning, he was medically treated and, in 2005, he was cured of lead poisoning, without any sequels, the fact that he suffered poisoning, as well as the behaviour assumed by the defendants after knowing the problem of lead poisoning, convinced the court of the responsibility of the defendants in this case. Indeed, the court understood that these offices did not take precautions in order to make sure that this problem would not arise. They waited for the problem to exist in order to take measures (when the harm was already done).

(2) According to the Law No. 16.112 of 30 May 1990, the Ministry of Housing, Land Demarcation and Environment has as a purpose – 'the establishment, execution and assessment of the national plans of protection of the environment and the instrumentation of the national policy in this matter'. Therefore, even though it was proven that the causes for this poisoning of the land were previous to the existence of this Ministry, according to the court, these conditions got worse during the time the Ministry existed, without it taking any measures in this matter.

(3) From the documents filed in the trial it can be concluded that since August of 2000, it was detected, in the low-income district called La Teja, lead poisoning in the children that lived there. This can be explained, among others, in the fact that in this area, a few years ago, there were smelting activities (and the Ministry did not prove to have controlled the persons that did this smelting activity either, in order to confirm that they proceeded with all the precautions required to protect the environment).

(4) However, the Municipality of Montevideo, according to its Organic Municipal Law no. 9515 (Article 35, numeral 24), was in charge of exercising the hygienic and sanitary police of the populations, resulting clear for the court that the Municipality omitted to comply with this obligation. This omission made the Municipality incur responsibility, even though after the news regarding lead poisoning were public, the Municipality, as well as the sued Ministry, took measures in order to minimize the damages.

Chapter 5. Others

§1. Strict Liabilities under the General Civil Code

I. Liability in Case of Damage Produced by Wild or Fierce Animals

438. As was already pointed out, Article 1329 of the CC establishes a strict liability in case of damage produced by wild or fierce animals. This article points out that:

> the damage caused by a wild or fierce animal, will always be attributable to whom has it under his care, notwithstanding if this person is his owner or not, and even if it was not possible for him to avoid the wrongdoing, and even if the animal had released itself without his fault.

439. The aforesaid will not be applicable to the authorities and public servants of the parks or State or municipal zoos to which what was established in the precedent article will not apply. The same rule will apply to the owners of private parks or zoos, their guardians and dependents in charge of watching the animals.

II. Strict Liability of the Manufacturer

440. The Civil Code, in its Article 1719, states that:

> the seller must repair the hidden defects, even though he ignored them, when an agreement establishing otherwise does not exist. The agreement in general terms, in virtue of which the seller will not respond for the hidden defects of the object, does not exempt him from liability for the hidden defect of which he was aware, and did not gave notice to the buyer. The same applies if the seller should have known of this defect due to his occupation or skills.

441. While Article 1721 of the Civil Code states:

> If the seller knew or should have known (Article 1719) of the hidden defects of the object sold and did not inform the buyer, the buyer will have, not only the option of the precedent article (to ask for the repair of the object sold) but also will have the right to be compensated of the damages suffered, if the buyer opts for the rescission of the contract.

442. Regarding this article, civil authors such as Jorge Peirano Facio have pointed out that:

> The profile of unlawfulness in the behaviour of the manufacturer is given by the manufacture of a defective product .... If the product has a defect, is

because the manufacturer has omitted the duties he has as such, that is, the duties of diligent manufacture, which constitutes the standard of his behaviour.[93]

443. Meanwhile, Professor Gamarra, citing Pothier, states that:

It is not, therefore, that the manufacturer is liable for a knowledge of the defect (because usually, he ignores it), but he is liable because his condition of manufacturer imposes him the guarantee of delivering to the market products without defects, and when his products have defects, he is liable forthe damages these products can cause. Seen this phenomenon in this way, it is the risk of the business, and not the guilt, the foundation of this liability.[94]

444. As it can be seen, both authors understand that in this case, we are before a case of strict liability, where the guilt is not needed to configure it. In the same line of thought, the Supreme Court, in its ruling 37/1993 dated 27 September 1993, established regarding the liability of the manufacturer the following:

a real strict liability, due to the hidden defect that exists even when the seller truly ignored the defect: the case that he should have known it due to his profession (…) The solution given in the contractual field is transferable to the extra-contractual field, due to the principle of the unity of the civil responsibility, or in virtue of the analogical interpretation accepted by Article 16 of the Civil Code.

§2. Other Strict Liabilities for Dangerous Activities

I. Strict Liability in Case of a Car Accident (SOA)

445. As was already pointed out, Law 18.412, referred to the SOA, is one of the cases of strict liability in Uruguay. Regarding this, the Second Civil Appellate Court stated in the ruling 124/2013, dated 21 August 2013, the following:

We are here under the regime of a strict liability, in which it is not taken into account nor investigated who was to be blamed for the accident, being enough to demonstrate the existence of the accident, that the vehicle intervened in it, and the damages suffered, in order for the claim to be admitted and the compensation to be ordered.

93. Jorge Peirano Facio, 'La responsabilidad civil del fabricante', Anuario de Derecho Comercial, number 4, p. 32.
94. Jorge Gamarra, 'Responsabilidad del fabricante', Anuario de Derecho Civil Uruguayo, Tomo XXVII, p. 233.

II. Strict Liability of the State in the Execution of Public Services

446. According to Article 24 of the Uruguayan Constitution, 'the State, the Departmental Governments, the Autonomous Entities, the Decentralized Services and, in general, any government body, will be civilly liable of the damage caused to third parties, in the execution of the public services trusted to its management or direction'.

447. Regarding this strict liability, ruling 721/1996 of the Supreme Court of Justice, stated in a case in which a bakery sued the State after a bus stop was changed of place, causing the reduction of the number of people that bought its products: 'the State will answer for every action that objectively causes harm to its inhabitants, i.e., regardless of the will of the State of causing it or not'.

448. Nevertheless, in this case, the court understood that the damage caused was not proven by the plaintiff. Regarding this, the court pointed out that:

> For this type of liability to exist, it is necessary that we are before an unlawful act of the Administration, case in which the principle that imposes compensation would apply. And although it is true that in some cases, even if the act of the Administration is lawful, it has to compensate for it anyways, the damage caused in this case has to be exceptional or uncommon.

449. Uruguayan authors also have written about this type of liability. One of the most important administrative lawyers of Uruguay, Professor Sayagues Laso, has pointed out the following: 'The damage suffered must be special, exceptional, surpass the normal sacrifices typical of life in society. If the law affected equally all or a great number of people, i.e., if in fact the effects were really general, there would be no obligation to compensate.'[95]

III. Strict Liability of the State for Wrongful Imprisonment

450. Article 4 of Law 15.859 states that:

> he who has suffered a preventive imprisonment in a criminal proceeding without having been condemned to a prison sentence for at least equal period of time to the time served, will have the right to receive a pecuniary compensation from the State, for the material damages, as well as for the pain and suffering that the preventive imprisonment, or the excess of it, had caused him. It is excluded from what was above mentioned, the cases of closing a procedure due to the death of the prisoner, waiver of the procedure by the accusing party, reduction of the sentence, elimination of the crime by a subsequent law to the prosecution, dismissal of the proceeding due to pardon or amnesty, as well as those in which the sentence is reduced due to the application of a more benign

95. Enrique Sayagués Laso, Tratado de Derecho Administrativo, Tomo. 1, p. 610.

law enacted after the prosecution and, in general, all the situations similar to the aforesaid. The compensation actions will be filed against the Tax Prosecutor on duty, and will be processed through the incidental proceeding. The State can then repeat what was paid against the third party responsible for the damage caused, according to the Constitution and the laws.

451. Regarding this liability, the Third Civil Appellate Court, in its ruling 60/2012 dated 3 December 2012, points out that:

> the claim filed referred to what is established in Article 4 of the Law 15.859, which first paragraph contains a special regulation of strict liability of the Estate regarding he who has not been sentenced to prison for a period at least equal to the one of the preventive imprisonment suffered. That is, if there was preventive imprisonment, but there was not a sentence, or while existing a sentence this was of a lesser period of imprisonment, due to this law the State is responsible without further analysis, unless in the cases of the second paragraph. Therefore, it is not possible to analyze the regularity of the jurisdictional acting. If the prisoner served preventive prison, and finally, was not sentenced to prison, or being sentenced to prison, the judge fixed an inferior period of imprisonment to the one already served, the State must compensate the prisoner, regardless of the conditions in which the sentence was issued.

452. In this case, a man of 45 years, without criminal records, that worked as a Commissioner (Chief Official), who unfairly served preventive imprisonment for almost five months, was compensated with USD 7,350 (plus interests from the time of the filing of the lawsuit).

IV. Strict Liability for the Damage Caused by a Fire Started by the Owner of a Field

453. Article 90 of the Uruguayan Rural Code (Law 10.024 enacted on the 14 June 1941), states that:

> Every owner can, under his responsibility, start a fire in his field, in order to clean it from weeds, insects or harmful animals, or for any other useful purpose, but if due to a sudden wind or due to a change of course of the wind, or due to any other guiltless or natural cause, fire exceeded its limits, and invaded other property, he will have to repair the damages caused. If an agreement is not signed, the damages will be fixed according to Article 47 (i.e., by experts appointed by both parties).

454. In reference to this liability, the Uruguayan Supreme Court, in its ruling 725/1996, dated 22 of July 1996, pointed out, in a case in which it was not proven by the plaintiff that the owner of the field was the one who started the fire and caused him damages, the following:

It is not enough that the owner be the guardian of the thing in order for the liability of the owner stated on Article 90 of the Rural Code to apply. The action of burning in this article, is clearly assigned to the owner, and although it is possible to understand reasonably comprised in the regulation the hypothesis of mediating an order of the owner, it does not correspond, conversely, to introduce in the strict liability the presumption of guardianship of the thing by the owner, applicable according to Article 1324 of the Civil Code, to the general regime of liability for the act of things.

V. Strict Liability for Customs Infractions

455. Article 287 of Act 13.318 states that:

> In the cases of customs violations, it will not be admissible any excuse founded on good faith, error committed by the infractor, or by someone else, or in the absence of intent of harming or defrauding the tax collector, notwithstanding what can be established by special laws.

456. Regarding this regulation, the Supreme Court, in ruling no. 367/2004 dated December 8, 2004, stated:

> Even though Article 287 of Law No. 13.318 establishes the principle of strict liability in the customs infractions, it is important to adopt a criterion of benignity or at least of flexibility to avoid excess in a rigid notion of the customs infractions.

VI. Strict Liability of Businessman, Distributors and other Professionals

457. The Consumer Protection Act (Law 17.250), enacted on 11 August 2000, states in Article 34 that:

> If from the defect or risk of the thing or service provided emerges damage to the consumer; the provider will be liable according to the regime established in the Civil Code (which, as we already saw, is one of strict liability for the manufacturer). The businessman or distributor will only be liable when the importer and manufacturer cannot be identified. In the same way, they will be liable if the damage is caused as a consequence of an inadequate preservation of the product, or when its original conditions are altered.

458. While Article 35 states that 'the liability of professionals will be a strict liability or a subjective one, depending on the nature of the service assumed' (e.g., when the final result is guaranteed, then we will be before a case of strict liability).

Part IV. Defences and Exemption Clauses

Chapter 1. Limitation of Action

§1. Statute of Limitations in Uruguayan Law

459. The CC, in its Articles 1215–1220, establishes rules for determining the cut-off dates after which it is too late for an intending plaintiff to bring a civil claim. This way, any civil claim, referred to as a right in rem, has a statute of limitations of twenty years, while any claim regarding the collection of debts has a statute of limitations of ten years. The right to start the execution process to collect the debt has a statute of limitations of five years (the statute of limitations was longer, but Law 19.889 dated 9 July 2020 shortened it).

460. The time for the statute of limitations to begin will start, in the conditional obligations, when the condition is accomplished, and in the obligations with a deadline, when the deadline comes. In the obligation of selling an object free from encumbrances, the statute of limitations will start at the time the encumbrances emerge. Regarding hidden defects, Article 1726 UCC states a statute of limitations of six months, and states that there will not be a liability for apparent defects. Nevertheless, the regulation for hidden and apparent defects in Law 17.250 is different. This will be analysed in point 478 and the following.

461. As regards the obligations with interests or fixed income, the statute of limitations will start from the last payment of interests or fixed income. When there is a court ruling, the period for the statute of limitations will start since the ruling became effective.

462. The CC also establishes what it calls short statutes of limitations, which are regulated from Article 1221 to Article 1227, and are the following:

(a) Claims against judges and lawyers, regarding the cases they had managed, can be filed for a period of five years.
(b) Claims regarding the duty to pay the construction or repair of middle walls and fences and constructions that are supported by middle walls can be filed for a period of five years from the date of the completion of the construction that originates this duty.

(c) Claims regarding the duty to pay the pavement tax of streets and roads have a statute of limitations of five years since the date in which the corresponding accounts were approved, or in its absence, when the public service was used by the public.

463. Meanwhile, the statute of limitations is of four years when it refers to the duty to pay the following arrears: arrears of alimony, arrears of the price of rent, arrears of interests of loans and arrears of all of which have to be paid in years or shorter periods (Article 1222 UCC).

464. The statute of limitation for cases of crimes or quasi-crimes is of four years. This period will start at the moment of the commitment of the crime or quasi-crime.

465. The statute of limitation will be of two years in the following cases (Article 1223 of the CC):

(i) Regarding the right of lawyers and other justice-related employees to collect their fees, rights and salaries. This period will start when the process is finished due to a ruling or an agreement between the parties or when the lawyer finishes rendering his services.
(ii) Regarding the fees of notaries. This period will start to run when the deed or legal document is executed.
(iii) In reference to the fees of doctors, surgeons, obstetricians and pharmacists, owed due to their visits, operations and medicines, this period will start to run when the medicines are delivered, or when the visits or operations are performed.
(iv) Regarding the owners of schools or hostels, the price of the pension or of the lessons.
(v) In reference to the shopkeeper and artisans, the price of their products, if the debtor lives in Uruguay. If he lives abroad, the period to file the claim will be of four years.
(vi) Regarding the salary of science or art teachers.

466. According to Article 1224, a mechanic will have one year to claim the price of his job (when this job is performed on a yearly basis). Innkeepers will have six months to file a claim to collect the price of the room and food provided monthly. Mechanics will also have six months to collect the price when their job is performed on a monthly basis.

467. In the last four cases aforementioned, the statute of limitations will continue to run, even though the services, work or provisions continued to be delivered or provided after the breach, and this period will only stop after the parties have given a written consent (in a public or private document) of the amount owed or if one party had given notice to the other party of a judicial proceeding, in which case the statute of limitations will become of ten years.

468. According to Article 1228 of the CC, felonies and their punishments will have the statute of limitations that the criminal law states. Also, the statute of limitations of the judicial deadlines and delays will be the ones established by the laws of civil and criminal proceedings.

469. The statute of limitations of months or years will be counted according to the Gregorian calendar.

§2. Interruption of the Statute of Limitations

470. According to Article 1233 of the CC, the statute of limitations can be subject to a natural or civil interruption.

471. The statute of limitations will be subject to a natural interruption in the following cases:

(i) When the owner of a right of way, after not using it for a while, starts using it before the statute of limitations has passed.
(ii) When the debtor acknowledges expressly or implicitly the existence of an obligation. In both cases, a new statute of limitations will begin.

472. The statute of limitations will be subject to a civil interruption after the possessor or the debtor are summoned. The conciliation court summons will also interrupt the statute of limitations from the day in which the summoning was served as long as, after thirty days from the day of the conciliation proceeding, the lawsuit is filed and served (Article 1236 of the CC).

473. The serving of the lawsuit, even if answered, will lose its effect, and will not interrupt the statute of limitations, if:

(i) the plaintiff withdraws from the lawsuit or the case finishes due to lack of interest of the parties to continue with it; or
(ii) the defendant is absolved from the complaint.

474. After the interruption takes place, the statute of limitations will start again. In cases of community property, any act that interrupts the statute of limitations will affect all owners.

475. The summoning performed to one of the debtors, or its acknowledgement of the debt, will affect all the other joint debtors and will interrupt the statute of limitations regarding them and their heirs (Article 1240 of the CC). The summoning of the main debtor, or his acknowledgement of the debt, will interrupt the statute of limitations also for the guarantor (Article 1241 of the CC).

§3. Suspension of the Statute of Limitations

476. According to Article 1242 of the CC, the statute of limitations will run against all kinds of persons unless the law states otherwise. Article 1243 establishes that the statute of limitations of three and ten years will be suspended in favour of:

(i) Minors, mentally impaired, deaf-mute who are unable to express themselves, and all of which are under parental authority or guardianship.
(ii) The inheritance is in abeyance, until an executor is appointed.

477. After the cause of suspension has ended, the statute of limitations will continue from where it was left off.

§4. Law 17.250: Consumer Protection Act

478. It is also important to point out that Articles 37–39 of Law 17.250 (called Consumer Protection Act) states a new statute of limitations for the contracts celebrated under the scope of this law. Therefore, this statute of limitations will apply to all contracts signed with consumers.

479. Article 37 establishes the following:

> The right to claim for apparent defects, or those of easy ascertainment, unless express acceptance of them, will expire:
> A) Thirty days, from the time in which the service or product was provided, if it referred to a short-lasting service or product,
> B) Ninety days, if the service or product was long-lasting.
> The statute of limitations will be counted from the moment in which the product was delivered, or the provision of the service finished. This period will be interrupted if the consumer files a claim duly documented before the supplier, and until the supplier unmistakably refuses this claim. In case of hidden defects, they will have to be evidenced in a period of six months and the statute of limitations will be of three months since these defects were noted; this, without prejudice of the existing legal provisions for some products and services.

480. Also, Article 38 of the law establishes that the cause of action to claim the compensation of the personal damages suffered will expire in a period of four years from the date in which the plaintiff had or should have had knowledge of the damage caused, or of the defect, and of the identity of the producer or manufacturer. This right will expire after a period of ten years after the date in which the supplier placed the product in the market or finished the provision of the service that caused damage.

481. According to Article 39 of the said law, the statute of limitations established in Articles 37 and 38 will be interrupted with the filing of the lawsuit, or with the notification of the conciliation process, as long as this is followed by a lawsuit within a period of thirty days after the conciliation audience.

Chapter 2. Grounds of Justification

§1. Consent

482. The victim's consent removes the unlawfulness of the offender's behaviour and excludes, therefore, the offender's liability. But the will of the victim is only suitable when the right is one that can be disposed of. Therefore, all injuries to patrimony can be subject to consent, but according to some authors, injuries to physical integrity or life cannot be consented to, due to the fact that they are excluded from commerce and that this would go against public order.

483. Nevertheless, it is important to point out that Article 44 of the CP authorizes consented injury.[96] Some examples given by Uruguayan authors regarding this consent is the case in which a person agrees to travel in a car where the driver is under the influence of alcohol or the case in which a person enters a private place with a sign of danger in the entrance.[97] Therefore, in these cases, the victim not only accepts the risks but also the possible harm.

484. This is different from the voluntary assumption of the risk by the victim. In this case, the situation has to comply with two requirements: (i) that the victim knows about the existing danger; and (ii) that the victim accepts it.

485. In the first case (consent of the victim), the victim accepts to suffer harm and, therefore, removes the unlawfulness of the tortfeasor's behaviour, while in the second case (acceptance of the risk by the victim), the consent refers only to the risk – not to the harm – and, therefore, the victim does not refuse to be compensated or wants the risk to become a reality. Therefore, here the person who causes the risk must act with diligence.

486. The acceptance of risks by the victim can give place to a total exoneration when the harm caused is due totally to the victim's guilt, or to a partial exoneration: when the offender acts also with guilt.

487. Nevertheless, if a person suffers harm while trying to save others, he will have the right to claim the compensation for this harm against those who caused the dangerous situation.[98]

§2. Necessity

488. Even though the CC does not refer to this ground of justification, Article 27 of the CP states:

96. Article 44 of the Uruguayan Criminal Code: 'An injury caused with the patients consent, is not punishable, unless this injury was caused to avoid the compliance of a law, or to cause harm to others.'
97. Gamarra, 'Tratado de Derecho Civil Uruguayo', Tomo XIX, *supra*, p. 227.
98. *Ibid.*, p. 229.

> He who, in order to defend his life, his physical integrity, his liberty, his reputation or his patrimony, attacks some of these rights belonging to others, as long as the harm caused is the same or lesser than the one that was sought to be avoided, that this harm was not provoked by his behavior and that it was both, imminent and unavoidable, will be exempt from liability. When the harm was caused to things, in order to prevent other harm to things, the harm caused must be lesser than the harm prevented. This Article is not applicable to he who has, legally, the duty to face this damage, nor to he who tried to prevent a damage that threatened third parties, unless these persons were his relatives in the grade established by numeral 2 of Article 26 (blood relatives which are direct relatives, or collateral relatives (until the second grade), the spouse, parents or children (acknowledged natural children or adopted).

489. This rule (which states the grounds of justification for a conduct) turns licit the behaviour of the tortfeasor and, therefore, authorizes it. In conclusion, this act would be part of the category of lawful acts that cause damage: it is lawful to cause harm to others when being in a state of necessity.

490. The state of necessity has been exemplified by some authors as the case in which a person driving a car has to change course in order to avoid running over a pedestrian and, due to this action, hits the glass window of a store, or the case in which a person uses other people's blankets in order to put down a fire.

491. This figure is similar to the force majeure or act of God. Indeed, in the case of an act of God, there is an irresistible force, while in the case of a state of necessity the person causing the damage is faced with an unavoidable damage. Nevertheless, the act of God intervenes in the causation of harm, while in the state of necessity causation is not questioned.

492. Regarding the compensation of the harm caused, civil authors understand the following: 'When the state of necessity is caused by a third party, this is the person that will have to compensate the harm done. If the state of necessity was caused by the fault of the tortfeasor, then he will have to compensate the damage caused.'

493. Gamarra understands that the person who suffered the harm, in case the tortfeasor acted in a state of necessity (and did not provoke it), can file a suit for unfair enrichment against the person that benefits from this harm.[99]

§3. Self-Help and Self-Defence

494. Although the CC does not refer to this ground of justification, the CP does.

99. *Ibid.*, 219–223.

495. Indeed, Article 26 of the CP states:

> The following are exempt from responsibility:1) He who acts defending himself or his rights or defending others, or others' rights, as long as the following happens: (i) An illegitimate aggression, (ii) the reasonable necessity of the means employed to repel or stop the harm. (iii) That the defender has not sufficiently provoked the attack. It will be understood that these three circumstances come together when a person defends or uses violence against a stranger who is found in his house or building. 2) The third requirement is not required when dealing with the defence of blood relatives which are direct relatives, or collateral relatives (until the second grade), of the spouse, parents or children (acknowledged natural children or adopted), as long as the defender has not taken part in the provocation of the harm. 3) When someone defends the person or rights of a stranger, he will also be exempt from responsibility, as long as circumstances of numeral 1 are met and that the defender is not driven by revenge, resentment or other illegitimate motive.

496. This rule, which states the grounds of justification for a conduct, as happens with the state of necessity, in this case, too, turns licit the behaviour of the tortfeasor and, therefore, authorizes it.

497. In conclusion, this act would also be part of the category of lawful acts that cause damage: it is lawful to cause harm to others when acting in self-defence or defending others.

498. Although this ground of justification is regulated by the CP, the Uruguayan Supreme Court acknowledged the application of this figure as a ground of justification in Civil law. Indeed, in its Ruling no. 304, dated 11 December 1974, the Supreme Court applied this figure to a man who defended himself with a punch from the armed aggression of another.[100]

§4. Others: Exercise of a Right

499. As was already pointed out in point 3 of Chapter 2, in Uruguayan law, the exercise of a right is also considered a ground of justification. Article 1321 of the CC states that 'he who uses his rights does not harm others'.

500. This article is not precise due to the fact that, sometimes, a person using a right causes harm to others. Someone can build his house and, during the construction, this will affect neighbours, who will have to deal with construction site dust and noise pollution. Nevertheless, if it is legal to build a house in that location, then the house owner will be acting according to law and, therefore, will not be liable for the nuisance caused.

---

100. *Ibid.*, pp. 219–220.

501. Therefore, the correct assertion would be to say that according to Uruguayan law, 'the harm produced as a consequence of the exercise of a right is protected by a ground of justification (to act according to law), which exonerates his author'.[101] Therefore, harm will be caused, but this damage will not be subject to compensation.

502. Notwithstanding this, an abuse of rights can happen when there is a deviation in the exercise of the right (regarding the interest pursued or the modality of its exercise). In case this happens, the author of the harm will have to compensate for it (this is analysed in point 3 of Chapter 2).

101. Gamarra & Gamarra, 'Responsabilidad Extracontractual', *supra*, p. 24.

Chapter 3. Contributory Fault

503. Part IV, Ch. 3, Contributory Fault One of the principal grounds of justification in Uruguayan law is the guilt of the victim. Notwithstanding the fact that the CC does not establish contributory fault as a ground of justification explicitly, no one challenges its viability nor its consequences, and the Civil Code in its Articles 1319 and 1331 contains this ground of justification implicitly.

504. Indeed, Article 1319 of the Civil Code, states that: 'Every unlawful act of men that causes harm to another, imposes to the individual whose wilful misconduct, fault or negligence has generated the harm, the duty to repair it (…)', while Article 1331 establishes the following: 'If a crime has been committed by two or more persons, each of them will have to answer jointly for the damage caused. This rule will not apply when the harm is produced by a quasi-crime. In this case, his authors will answer proportionally.'

505. From these articles, it can be concluded that a person must answer for the harm he caused. Therefore, if part of the harm was caused by the victim, this part of the harm will not have to be compensated (the compensation will be proportional to the part of the harm caused).

506. For the offender to be exonerated of part of the guilt, the act that caused harm cannot have been provoked by him.

507. In Uruguay, the jurisprudence usually attributes to the victim a lesser percentage of the guilt than the one he should have. It has been understood that, in cases of run over, the reason for this is that the percentage of the harm attributed to the victim will go uncompensated, while the one attributed to the offender will be paid by the insurance company.

508. In Uruguayan jurisprudence, many cases of guilt of the victim can be found, especially in transit accidents. In these cases, this exemption or reduction on the participation in the harm has been applied: when the victim crossed the street in the middle of the block (and not using the cross-walk) or when the victim crosses the street without looking or is under the influence of alcohol or other drugs.

509. Uruguayan authors have also analysed the situation in which an individual legally incapacitated contributes to the harm he experiences. The majority of the authors understand that in these cases, the offender will only have to answer for part of the harm (according to the percentage of guilt he had in the accident). Also, in cases in which a person is following instructions, jurisprudence has understood that the victim did not act with fault. Indeed, the Supreme Court of Justice, in its ruling 1/2018, dated 2/1/2018, stated the following: 'The Appellate Court was wrong when it understood that the harm occurred due to the fault of the victim. Although as an executive policeman he was not obliged to unload bikes from a truck, he acted complying with an order, and that is what caused him the harm suffered. The act of unloading the bikes was not voluntary, but performed in compliance with an express order.'

Chapter 4. Exemption Clauses

510. Exemption clauses are used in contracts in order to limit a party's responsibility. Due to the fact that this type of clauses have been used to beneficiate the strong party in a contract, to the detriment of the weaker party, the Consumer Protection Act (Law No. 17.250) published on 17 August 2000, states in its Article 31 the following:

> Among others, the following are considered abusive clauses:
> A) Clauses that exempt from liability or limit the liability of the supplier, for the defects of any nature, of the products or services, unless law allows it or unless, due to any other cause, this exemption is justified.
> B) Clauses that imply a waive of rights of the consumer.
> C) Clauses that authorize the supplier to modify the terms of the contract.
> D) The resolutory clause agreed exclusively in favor of the supplier.
> E) The clauses which impose the burden of proof in the consumer, when legally it corresponds to the supplier.
> F) Clauses which impose representatives to the consumer.
> G) Clauses on virtue of which the consumer waives his right to be compensated or reimbursed of any expenditure which legally correspond to the supplier.
> H) Clauses that state that the silence of the consumer will be taken as acceptance of any modification, restriction or extension of what was agreed in the contract.
> I) Clauses that state the automatic renewal of the contract, without allowing the consumer to put an end to the contract without liability. The consumer, in a period of 60 days after the automatic renewal took place, can inform the supplier of his intention of not continuing with the contract, with a prior notice of 15 days.
>
> The inclusion of abusive clauses to the contract gives the consumer the right to ask for the annulment of them, in which case the Judge will have to integrate the contract. If after doing so, the Judge understands that the contract lacks consideration, he can declare the nullity of the contract.

511. Notwithstanding this, before the enactment of this law, the Supreme Court have already pronounced about this in some cases in which the supplier of products or services, introduced in the contract an exemption clause, or made an exemption announcement to whom it may concern, and declared that in these cases these exemptions would not be valid unless a just cause justified it (as it could be, the reduction of the price in exchange of the assumption of risks by the other party). This is the case of the garage contract, and of the lodging contract, among others.

512. Indeed, authors have established that in the lodging contract, the innkeeper cannot exempt himself from liability by making a general announcement to guests, for example, by hanging a sign with the announcement on the wall.[102]

513. Regarding the garage contract, jurisprudence in Uruguay has determined that, in general, clauses exempting or limiting liability are not acceptable because they break the contractual balance, for example, 'the garage will not be liable for damages caused by fire'. But authors understand that this must be analysed on a case-by-case basis because it would be possible for a garage to be exempt from liability if previously an agreement is signed between the parties in which the price is reduced and the car owner accepts the assumption of the risks regarding force majeure.[103]

102. Venturini, Beatriz and others, 'Manual de Contratos II', article written by Beatriz Venturini and Mariana Barúa, 1st ed., Editorial UM Universidad de Montevideo, January, 2004, Montevideo, p. 215.
103. Venturini et al., 'Manual de Contratos II', article written by Beatriz Venturini and Mariana Barúa, *supra*, p. 218.

Part V. Causation

514. According to Article 1319, 'Every unlawful act of men that cause harm to another, imposes to the individual whose wilful misconduct, fault or negligence has generated the harm, the duty to repair it ....'

515. Causation will refer to the imputation of the harm. This imputation can be a material imputation, which is the only one needed when the responsibility has an objective nature, or it can also be psychological, which is needed when fault also has to be proven.[104]

516. There are four theories that try to determine the way causation must be established:

(i) *Theory of the equivalence of the conditions:* This theory understands that when a situation or a conduct occurs and is imputable to several persons that acted at the same time or one after the other, all of them must be responsible if all of these conducts were needed for the harm to be caused. This theory is criticized, because in some cases a specific harm can happen due to infinite causes, extending, therefore, the responsibility regime in a way which is excessive and unacceptable. Also, this theory would imply that any of the persons intervening in the harm would be responsible to compensate for all of it because if its conducts had not happened, the harm would not exist. This is expressly forbidden by Article 1331 of the Civil Code, which states that in case of quasi-crimes, performed by several persons, responsibility must be proportional to the participation in the harm.

(ii) *Theory of the cause and the occasion (condition):* This theory points out that it is important to differentiate the real cause of the harm, from the previous acts that allowed the real cause to happen but did not cause it.

(iii) *Theory of the efficient cause and the close cause:* This theory normally applies when there are causes for the harm that exclude the others. This theory tries to limit the responsibility to those causes closely related to the final harm (the closer in time and space). Authors criticize this theory, saying that its only usefulness is to establish a guidance in order not to extend disproportionately, in time and space, the influence of other factors. The weakness of this theory lies in the fact that not always the closest cause of harm is the only one that causes it. In this respect, Gamarra comments that even though the close cause theory

104. Gamarra & Gamarra, 'Responsabilidad Extracontractual', *supra*, p. 41.

is not accepted by jurisprudence, in France, even though this theory is rejected, judges give preference to the closest cause, in the process of considering the cause of harm, because, normally, this is the one that causes it.

(iv) *Theory of the adequate causation:* This theory is the one currently applied by most jurisprudence. It states that the cause of harm consists in the event that normally causes this consequence. The cause to be adequate must be probable, regular and reasonably predictable. This theory selects from all the events that happened before the harm was caused, the ones that were just precedents, from those that were causes of it. Nevertheless, this rule has an exception. When the defendant has shown a deliberate intention to commit a wrongful act (malice), then he will have to compensate for exceptional damage (the one which is not probable or predictable).

Part VI. Remedies

Chapter 1. General Principles

517. In Uruguayan law, there are three rules which are used to analyse and value damages.[105] The first rule is Article 1319 of the Civil Code, which states that: 'Every unlawful act of men that causes harm to another imposes to the individual whose wilful misconduct, fault or negligence has generated the harm, the duty to repair it. (…)'

518. The second rule that helps value damages is Article 1323 of the Civil Code, which states that: 'The damage comprises not only the harm directly caused but also the lost profits which are an immediate consequence of the unlawful act.'

519. Finally, Article 1346 of the Civil Code establishes that: 'the debtor will not answer but for the damages that were foreseen, or could have been foreseen at the time of the contract, when he has not acted with malice when breaching the contract'.

520. Even in case the debtors breach was due to malice, damages that are not established by law or agreed by the parties, will not comprise, regarding the loss suffered by the creditor and the profit he was deprived of, but what was an immediate and direct consequence of the breach. As can be seen, the rules regarding this matter are few, and therefore, most of the information referred to the analysis and value of damages is created by doctrine and jurisprudence.

105. Jorge Gamarra, 'Tratado de Derecho Civil Uruguayo', Tomo XXIII, Editorial Fundación de Cultura Universitaria, Montevideo, 2007, pp. 18–22.

Chapter 2. Kinds of Damage

§1. Individual and Collective Damage

521. To establish if we are before an individual or a collective damage, it has to be determined what prevails: the damage to a certain person or group of persons that can be easily compensated or a damage inferred to a group or community, where the compensation is difficult to fix.

522. The collective damage does not emerge from the sum of individual damages, it presents autonomy, because it affects, at the same time, the group or community which is a victim of this damage.

523. Collective damages usually occur in the case of environmental damages, nuclear damages, and damages generated by a defective product introduced in the market, among others.

524. The injured parties of this damage are not people separately identified, but certain categories or classes, linked by a specific circumstance which makes them victims of this damage.[106]

525. While individual damage is the one regulated by the Civil Code, mentioned in the precedent chapter, collective damage, in Uruguay, is regulated by Article 42 of the General Procedure Code.

526. This article states that, in issues related to the defence of the environment, the cultural or historical values and, in general, those that belong to an indeterminate group of persons, the people that will have legal standing to promote an action will be, interchangeably, the Public Prosecutor, any interested party or the organizations or associations of social interest that, according to the law or an opinion of the court, guarantee a proper defence of the interest involved.

527. Regarding what is established in this article, even though civil authors agree that it regulates the diffuse interests, it is not clear if it also regulates collective interests. In this respect, Uruguayan litigation law professors, such as Fernando Cardinal and Selva Klett, have expressed that the legislator, when writing this law, only pointed out that the regulated interests had to belong to an indeterminate group. Also, they point out that the collective interests are comprised, as well as the diffuse interests, not because they are collective but due to the indetermination of the persons who belong to this group. Indeed, if the members of a group were not easy to

106. Garrido Cordobera, 'Los Daños Colectivos y la Reparación', Editorial Universidad, 1993, Buenos Aires, pp. 92–93.

identify, to require the attendance of all of them in the procedure in a joint litigation would be the equivalent to deny them justice.[107]

§2. Direct and Indirect Damage

528. In Uruguay, in contractual liability, the only damage that is mandatory to compensate is the one which is an immediate and direct consequence of the breach. Indeed, Article 1346 of the Civil Code establishes that the debtor will not answer but for the damages that were foreseen, or could have been foreseen at the time of the contract when he has not acted with malice when breaching the contract.

529. And after this, it states that even in case the debtors breach was due to malice, damages that are not established by law or agreed by the parties will not comprise the loss suffered by the creditor and the profit he was deprived of, but what was an immediate and direct consequence of the breach.

530. Regarding extra-contractual liability, Article 1323 of the Civil Code states that the damage comprises not only the harm directly caused but also the lost profits which are an immediate consequence of the unlawful act. Therefore, in case of extra-contractual liability, the harm to be compensated, as well as in contractual liability, will only be the one that was a direct consequence of the unlawful act.

§3. Pecuniary and Non-pecuniary Losses

531. The pecuniary damage manifests in two ways: (i) the pecuniary losses (called *daño emergente*), which Article 1323 refers to as the harm directly caused, and Article 1346 refers to as the loss suffered; and (ii) the lost profits (called *lucro cesante*), which Article 1323 refers to as the lost profits and Article 1346 as the profit the creditor was deprived of.

532. The main difference between the pecuniary losses and the lost profits is that in the first case the harmed party suffers a reduction in his estate or has to pay expenses as a consequence of the accident or breach ('a positive loss'), while in the loss of profits there is a 'negative loss', which consists in the loss of profits that the damaged party would have generated in the future if the damage had not occurred.[108]

533. The non-pecuniary losses, in Uruguay, belong to the notion called *daño moral* (moral damage), which would be the equivalent to pain and suffering. This

107. Mariana Barúa, 'Legitimación Activa de Cualquier Interesado para Actuar en Representación de Intereses Difusos o Colectivos', Publisher in the Uruguayan Newspaper Ultimas Noticias, on 5 Nov. 2009.
108. Gamarra, 'Tratado de Derecho Civil Uruguayo', Tomo XXIII, *supra*, pp. 18–22.

damage is not regulated by the CC, but jurisprudence considers it a kind of damage that, if proven, must be compensated by the tortfeasor or breaching party.

§4. Pure Economic Loss

534. As was already mentioned in Chapter 1 of part VI, pure economic loss is regulated in our legislation, as pecuniary losses and lost profits, in Articles 1323 and 1346 of the CC.

§5. Actual and Future Damage (Lost Profits)

535. The damages that a person can suffer through time can vary. Because of these, damages can be classified in the present and the future. Authors understand that it is not exact to affirm that pecuniary losses are the same as past or actual damage and that loss of profits is the same as future damages. This can be explained by the fact that some pecuniary losses can appear after the damage was caused (e.g., in case sometime after a car accident, the person needs new surgical operations due to new complications caused by the car accident suffered), while lost profits can already occur (and probably will have occurred already, due to the duration of the procedure), when the judge rules.[109]

536. There are three moments when damages can be analysed by the judge: (i) at the time in which they were inferred; (ii) at the time of the lawsuit; and (iii) at the time of the ruling. Regarding this, jurisprudence understands that the proper moment to analyse the damages suffered will be at the time of the ruling. The ruling in favour of the plaintiff can order the compensation of present damages as well as of future damages (those that will occur after the final sentence).

537. Professor Berdaguer[110] defines future damages as those damages that having originated before the final ruling will produce its negative consequences in the future. Also, Professor Calvo Costa[111] points out that the future damage appears as the extension or aggravation of the actual damage, but will still keep a causality connection with it. Finally, Professor Juan Espinoza Espinoza[112] says that the future damage can be defined as any consequence with a negative impact that occurs after the judicial procedure.

---

109. *Ibid.*, p. 21.
110. Jaime Berdaguer, Consultation dated 12 May 2010, filed in a case of civil liability before the 9th Civil District Court, in the case 'Rodriguez Carril, Sylvana Sabrina and others *v.* Pressa, Carlos and others. Damages' (file 2-3625/2010), p. 7.
111. C. Calvo Costa, 'Daño resarcible', Bs. As. (2005), p. 250, citado por Berdaguer, Jaime, *supra*, p. 7.
112. Juan Espinoza Espinoza, 'Derecho de la Responsabilidad Civil', 2º Edición Actualizada y Aumentada, Editorial Gaceta Jurídica, Lima, 2003, p. 190.

538. From what was said, it could be concluded that the future damage is the damage that occurs after the judicial procedure, but that generates due to the unlawful act that gave place to it. In order for this damage to be compensated, according to Salvi,[113] the future damage must have expressed some signs from which it could be reasonably foreseen that it would emerge.

539. Regarding this issue, Professor Gamarra[114] understands that a judge can sentence to compensate future damages, as long as the judge can foresee with relative certainty that these damages will occur.

§6. Other Costs

540. It is important to point out that, in Uruguay, the rule is that each party pays its own legal costs. These costs refer to legal fees, court costs, the cost of hiring experts (which can be hired by the parties, or appointed by the court) and the cost of obtaining proof (which sometimes refers to declarations that have to be drafted by public notaries), among others.

541. Notwithstanding this, there are some cases in which the law establishes the obligation of one of the parties to pay the legal fees and court costs.

542. The second and third paragraph of Article 688 of the CC states that the judge can abstain from ordering special condemnation in court costs or order the defeated party to pay court costs, and even that the court can condemn the defeated party to pay court costs and the legal fees of the opposing party, depending on whether the judge understands that the defeated party acted with some reason or with guilty glibness or with malice that deserves the note of recklessness, notwithstanding what procedural law establishes.

543. Court costs will comprise all the taxes, including the payment of the tax referred to legal fees, as well as the fees of the experts, custodians, appraisers and the other assistants of the court.

544. Legal fees will comprise the fees of the lawyers and advanced law students.

545. Article 56.1 of the General Procedure Code states that 'the final ruling will condemn to the payment of court costs, legal fees or will declare that there is no reason for a special condemnation, according to what is established in Article 688 of the Civil Code'.

113. Salvi, voz Risarcimento del danno, en Enciclopedia del Diritto XL, Giuffre, Milano, 1989, p. 1090, citado por Juan Espinoza Espinoza, *supra*, p. 190.
114. Gamarra, 'Tratado de Derecho Civil Uruguayo', Tomo XXIII, *supra*, p. 37.

546. Article 56.2 of the General Procedure Code states that the regime established in the precedent numeral will be applied to all the legal actions contained in this Code, except the following proceedings: executive proceeding, execution proceeding, proceeding of delivery of a thing, cassation, request for review and unconstitutionality of laws. In these procedures, the special regime established for each of these proceedings by the General Procedure Code will apply.

547. Finally, Article 56.3 states that the party, to whom the Court ruled in favour, sentencing the other party to pay the court costs and the legal fees, will file a calculation of what is owed due to these concepts, before the court clerk, who will approve or correct it and will issue a document which will allow the party to start an execution procedure for the collection of those costs. The calculation will be notified to the other party and it can be appealed before the court, which will issue a final ruling in this regard.

548. Also, it is important to point out that some of the regulations that establish the obligation to pay court costs and legal fees, without requiring that the party acts with glibness or malice, are the following:

(i) *Condemnation in the Incidences*: Article 57 of the General Procedure Code states that the ruling that decides about the incidences will order the defeated party the payment of the court costs, notwithstanding the possibility to order too the payment of the legal fees, if it corresponded according to Article 688 of the Civil Code (guilty glibness or malice). The second instance ruling, if confirmed entirely, will impose mandatorily the condemnation in court costs and legal fees unless the court refuses to this on good grounds.

(ii) *Defendant Acquiesce to the claim*: Article 58 of the General Procedure Code establishes that when, from the records of the procedure, it can be appreciated that the defendant acquiesced to the claim during the time to answer it and that he did not give a reason for the lawsuit to be filed, the plaintiff will be condemned to pay all the court costs and legal fees of the procedure. It will also be possible to condemn the plaintiff to pay these costs when the defendant had partially acquiesced to the claim, and the sentence only accepts this part of the claim.

(iii) *Voluntary dismissal*: Article 231 of the General Procedure Code points out that in the cases of waiver of the right, application for voluntary dismissal of procedure, of the action, of the objection or of the appeal, the party which applied for voluntary dismissal will pay the court costs, notwithstanding the condemnation in legal fees if it corresponded (Article 688 of the Civil Code: guilty glibness or malice), unless otherwise agreed by the parties.

(iv) *Complaint for denial of an Appeal*: Article 267 of the General Procedure Code establishes that the court costs and legal fees of the complaint to the court, for the denial of an appeal, will be imposed according to Article 57 (they will have to be paid by the defeated party) and will benefit the other party, as long as she intervened.

(v) *Cassation*: Article 279 of the General Procedure Code states that the court costs and legal fees of the cassation will be imposed according to what is established in Article 56.1 (in general, each party will have to pay his legal costs).

(vi) *Revision appeal before the Supreme Court*: Article 292 of the General Procedure Code points out that the court costs and legal fees of the revision appeal before the Supreme Court, that was not admitted, will be paid by the appellant. If the revision appeal was admitted, the Supreme Court of Justice will only condemn mandatorily the defeated party if he had participated in the acts that determined the revocation of the ruling. In the rest of the cases, the imposition of court costs and legal fees will be determined according to circumstances.

(vii) *Non-attendance to a preliminary diligence*: Article 310.2 of the General Procedure Code states that in the preliminary diligence, if the party who asked for it did not attend the audience, he will be deemed desisted from his petition, condemning him to the payment of court costs and legal fees unless he could not attend due to an act of God, in which case, this hearing can be postponed for one time.

(viii) *Preliminary diligences in court*: Article 310.4 of the General Procedure Code points out that if the preliminary diligence was performed despite the opposition of the party against which it was asked, court costs and legal fees will be paid by each party unless this opposition was made with malice, which resulted in recklessness that postponed the diligence in an unduly and extended way.

(ix) *Executive Procedure*: Article 354.1 of the General Procedure Code states that in an executive procedure, the court will order immediately the seizure and will condemn the defendant to the payment of the quantity claimed, plus interests, legal fees and court costs.

(x) *Admission of motion of incompetence*: Article 359 of the General Procedure Code establishes that if the sentence admitted the motion of incompetence, the court will order the plaintiff to pay the court costs, and will order that the file goes to the competent court for the decision of the case.

(xi) *Defeated party in an execution procedure*: Article 392.1 of the General Procedure Code points out that the executed party (in a procedure of execution) will have to pay for the court costs and legal fees and the other justified expenses for the execution of the sentence.

(xii) *Revocation of Insolvency Trial*: Article 458.6 of the General Procedure Code establishes that the sentence that revokes the insolvency trial will reinstate things as they were before the declaration and can impose the creditors that asked for the insolvency trial, the payment of legal fees and costs, including the fees of the liquidator.

(xiii) *Unconstitutionality Action*: Article 523 states that when an action of unconstitutionality is not admitted and it was filed by an interested party, the party who filed the action will have to pay the court costs, and the legal fees, when according to Article 688 of the Civil Code, it corresponds. This article also points out that it will be considered that recklessness malice exists when the proposal of the issue at hand showed clearly that the purpose of this action was to retard the respective procedures. In this last case, the attorney that advised the plaintiff will lose his right to legal fees.

(xiv) *Eviction*: Article 1706 of the CC states that when a person agrees to deliver a property free from encumbrances and hidden defects, and then the purchaser suffers eviction, then the purchaser can demand the seller, among others, the reimbursement of the legal fees and costs of the trial.

§7. Mitigation of Damages

549. The duty to mitigate damages and its consequences is a duty of the creditor in the contractual field as well as in extra-contractual cases. In this regard, civil authors, as well as jurisprudence, have understood that this duty derives from the application of the general principle that requires acting with good faith.

550. The duty to mitigate damages implies that the victim of a damage derived from an unlawful act should not sit by without taking measures to minimize the damage and its consequence, with the purpose of claiming, afterwards, a bigger compensation for the damages suffered. On the contrary, the creditor of compensation has an obligation to take all reasonable measures that are at his disposal in order to neutralize the damage or minimize its effects.[115]

551. Our country ratified the Vienna Convention on the International Sale of Goods (1980). In its Article 77, it expressly states that 'the party that alleges the breach of the contract shall adopt all the reasonable measures, considering the circumstances, in order to reduce the loss, including the loss of profits, resulting from the breach. If he does not take all the measures, the counterparty can ask that the compensation for damages is reduced in the amount in which the loss should have been reduced'.

552. It is discussed if the duty to mitigate damages refers to a problem of good faith or if it also refers to the lack of appropriate cause. The latter, because the omissive behaviour of the victim contributes to the aggravation of the damage, therefore, would interrupt the appropriate cause between the breach of the debtor and the magnitude of the damages. The same reasoning is valid in extra-contractual matters when the victim of an injury caused by a road traffic accident omits to perform the healing process that the doctor orders and then, for example, loses a leg due to an infection. In this case, the magnitude of the damage will not have appropriate cause with the unlawful act of the driver but will have as cause the victims' behaviour, who omitted the minimum diligence in the healing process.[116]

---

115. Gonzalo Ramírez, 'La codicia y la buena fe', article publisher in the digital version of the Uruguayan newspaper 'El Pais', which can be found at http://www.elpais.com.uy/economia-y-mercado/codicia-buena-fe.html.

116. *Ibid.*

553. *553.* The Vienna Convention, in its Article 85, regulates a similar situation but refers to the mitigation of damages behaviour that a seller of merchandise must adopt when the buyer does not show on time to withdraw it or does not pay the price in order to be legitimated to take it. In this case, the seller cannot let the merchandise spoil in his warehouse without taking any measures. He must preserve this merchandise and, eventually, sell it in the market.

554. The right criteria to determine the reach of the duty to mitigate damages is given by the principle of reasonability. Indeed, the creditor does not have the duty to perform an extraordinary effort to minimize the damages or assume an extraordinary debt in order to make up for the breach of his debtor, putting in risk his own patrimony, but he has to take all the measures that are within his reach that allow a reasonable mitigation of damages.

Chapter 3. Assessment and Compensation of Damages

§1. Objective Versus Subjective

555. Under Uruguayan tort law, there are no rules for the assessment of damages. Judges must establish the amount of them according to their understanding and experience. Notwithstanding this, there are some rules that judges must apply.

556. Article 139.1 of the General Procedure Code states that he who has a pretention about something has the burden of proof of the facts he alleges, and he who contradicts what is alleged has the burden of proof regarding the modifying, deterrent or extinctive facts.

557. Therefore, if a plaintiff asks for a compensation for damages suffered, he must add to his lawsuit the proof of the suffering of these damages (which can be documents, witness testimonies, expert reports, documents from the third parties, etc.).

558. Now, again, jurisprudence has understood that, sometimes, it is not necessary to prove the damages because judges can infer them by analysing the circumstances of the breach or accident. Indeed, judges have understood that taxi expenses as well as food and accommodation expenses, when the treatment for the injuries has to be performed far from home, can be presumed.[117]

559. Therefore, it could be said that judges, according to Uruguayan law, must fix the amount of the compensation according to what was proved by the plaintiff (objective criterion), but sometimes, in order to fix them, in the absence of clear proof, or when dealing with pain and suffering damages, they can use a subjective criterion (called maxims of experience).

560. Notwithstanding this, since 1980, judges have decided to apply the empiric criterion to the compensations referred to pain and suffering damages. Since then, when the judges rule, they mention the precedent rulings they use as a guide to establish a certain amount of compensation. Appeal Courts started drafting their own scale of compensations, in order to use it as a guide.

561. In 1985, Beatriz Venturini published the first scale of compensation for pain and suffering,[118] which brought appreciation of the amounts managed to compensate for different scenarios. The main critic of this scale was that the compensations were very low.

---

117. Gamarra, 'Tratado de Derecho Civil Uruguayo: La Reparación del Perjuicio', Tomo XXIII, *supra*p. 55.
118. Anuario de Derecho Civil Uruguayo, Tomo XV, Editorial Fondo de Cultura Universitaria, Montevideo, p. 130.

562. This scale was enlarged with new data and published in Judge Beatriz Venturini's book 'El Daño Moral' (Pain and Suffering Damages),[119] which had a great repercussion in subsequent jurisprudence. This way, although Uruguayan courts are not bounded by precedent rulings, with the establishment of this rule, they auto-limit themselves in the interest of fairer rulings.[120]

§2. Concrete Versus Abstract

563. This is linked with the above classification of damages. Concrete damages refer to those damages subject to proof. Regarding them, the plaintiff must prove the damage suffered, as well as the amount of this damage, and the judge, for its quantification, will apply an objective criterion.

564. Nevertheless, to fix the value of a concrete damage can sometimes be difficult because of the sentimental value that things might entail. Maybe a diamond ring costs USD 1,000, but if it was a ring which belonged to the great-grandmother and has been for centuries in the family, the value of this object cannot be reduced to its market value.

565. Meanwhile, the injured party's abstract damages refer to the pain and suffering damages. These damages cannot be measured with an objective criterion, and regarding them, the judge must apply a subjective criterion in order to fix the amount for their compensation.

566. Nevertheless, as was already mentioned, currently, judges use a scale for the compensations ordered for pain and suffering, in order to determine the compensation they will order in a specific case. Also, since 1980, when judges rule, they mention the precedent rulings they use as a guide to establish a certain amount of compensation.

§3. Methods of Assessing Damage

567. As was already said, Uruguayan law states that the wrongdoer must compensate the victim for the material damages suffered as well as for the lost profits (Articles 1323 and 1346 of the CC). Although not expressly established, Uruguayan doctrine and jurisprudence understand that pain and suffering damages are also subject to compensation.

568. Regarding contractual liability, the debtor that did not act with malice will be liable only for the damages that were foreseen, or could have been foreseen at

119. Beatriz Venturini, 'El Daño Moral', Editorial Fundación de Cultura Universitaria, Montevideo, 2d ed., 1992, p. 103.
120. Jorge Gamarra, 'Tratado de Derecho Civil Uruguayo: La Reparación del Perjuicio', Tomo XXV, Montevideo, 2005, p. 436.

the time of the contract, while the debtor that acted with malice will have to compensate for all the damages (even those that could not be foreseen) as long as they are an immediate and direct consequence of the breach.

569. The burden of proving the amount for damages corresponds to the victim, but sometimes the judges can order compensation for damages that were not proved if they understand that the existence of those damages can be presumed.

570. Regarding pain and suffering damages, judges use a scale to fix the amount of these damages and mention the precedent rulings they use as a guide to establish a certain amount of compensation. Also, it is understood in Uruguayan jurisprudence that for pain and suffering damages to be admitted, they must be serious and must not account for temporary discomfort.

§4. Equitable Limitations of Damages

571. Uruguayan tort law does not include a general rule which allows the court to reduce the compensation amount when a behaviour causes an excessive damage to a person who is in a better position to bear it.

572. But taking into account that judges in Uruguay can apply a subjective criterion, it is common that in cases like these, judges analyse the circumstances in which damages were caused in order to mitigate the compensation amount.

§5. Methods of Payment

I. Lump Sum

573. In Uruguay, judges order equal amount of compensations as lump sums and compensations with annuities. It cannot be said that one of these options prevail. If, in a case in which future damages are claimed, a judge adopts the lump sum method, he will analyse statistically which amount he should fix now in order to cover the damages the plaintiff will suffer in the future.

574. Jurisprudence understands that what is asked for in the lawsuit, or what parties might agree to, obliges the court. Therefore, if the plaintiff asks for compensation through a lump sum, judges cannot order the payment of annuities or periodical payments.

575. This was analysed by the Seventh Civil Appeal Court in its ruling dated 17 September 1986, in which the Court of Appeals revoked a sentence of the District Court because it fixed the compensation through a monthly payment when the plaintiff asked in his lawsuit for a lump sum.

576. Notwithstanding this, in some cases doctrine and jurisprudence have understood that due to the case in hand; the method of payment asked for by the plaintiff can be disregarded. This happens, for example, in the cases where the plaintiffs are minors represented by their parents or older people or people with mental incapacities that would not be able to administer a lump sum of money.[121]

577. Civil authors have said that the disadvantage of the lump sum is that it can be rapidly squandered and, afterwards, the victim would become a burden to society. The advantage of this method is that it provides a quick solution for the payment issue and allows the debtor to free himself from liability.

578. This solution is preferred by the victims, and by the insurance companies, that wish to close the case once and for all. When the victim asks for the payment of future damages, such as lost salaries, it is common that judges apply to this amount claimed the financial mathematics formula in virtue of which the capital fixed now will have into account the interests it will generate in the future.

579. Regarding this matter, the Supreme Court has said in a ruling, dated 30 September 1998, that financial mathematics must be applied to the amounts that refer to condemnations for the future because 'it would be excessive to order the payment of a lump sum initially representative of the loss suffered without taking into account the interests that this amount will produce to the plaintiff'.

II. Annuities

580. It is common for Uruguayan judges to order the payment of annuities. The advantage of an annuity is that it provides security to the injured party who has the certainty of a fixed periodical deposit that he will receive, sometimes, for the rest of his life.

581. Also, the economic benefit will remain unchanged during the time it is claimable because it will be constantly adjusted. Periodical payment rules out the possibility of squandering the compensation received, protecting the victim from its own inexperience or unskillfulness of administering large sums of money and also protecting them from unscrupulous third parties.

582. Also, this method of payment is the most convenient for damages that continue emerging in the future. Also, if the victim dies shortly after the final ruling, the compensation will have paid the actual damages and the victim's heirs will not unduly benefit from a large lump sum.[122]

---

121. Jorge Gamarra, 'Tratado de Derecho Civil Uruguayo: La Reparación del Perjuicio. Vol 2.', Tomo XXIV, Editorial Fondo de Cultura Universitaria, Montevideo, 1992, p. 392.
122. Gamarra, 'Tratado de Derecho Civil Uruguayo', Tomo XXIV, *supra*, pp. 391–399.

III. Others

583. Not always the method of periodical payment of money is annual; it could be monthly or half-yearly.

Chapter 4. Personal Injury and Death

§1. Pecuniary Losses

584. After a person suffers a personal injury or dies, he or his heirs can ask for compensation for the medical and other expenses related to the healing process as well as for the lost earnings.

585. If the injured party dies or becomes incapacitated and he is or was a social security beneficiary, this State body will pay him or his heirs a monthly fixed amount of money and, afterwards, will repeat this amount from the tortfeasor.

586. The Health Maintenance Organization (HMO) that attended the injured party also have the right to repeat against the tortfeasor for all the expenses the medical treatment cost them.

§2. Non-pecuniary Losses

587. Although the Civil Code does not refer to pain and suffering damages, Uruguayan doctrine and jurisprudence understand compensation for this damage must be admitted. The different categories that have been analysed under this damage refer to the following.

I. Damage to the Relationship

588. This damage was considered for the first time in 1960 and refers to the damages caused by the victim that are not related to labour issues. This damage comprises aesthetic damage, sexual damage and youthful damage.

589. The aesthetic damage refers to the damage caused to a victim when the unlawful act leaves durable trails that aesthetically affect the victim (such as scars, deformations, etc.)

590. The sexual damage refers to the damage that affects the satisfaction of physiological necessities and the impossibility to procreate (infertility).

591. Finally, the youthful damage is defined as a damage to the childhood and youth and is found in the idea that the loss of the physical integrity is most vividly suffered by a young man than by an elderly man; these people will be deprived of the activities common for their age, such as practising sports, attending dances, etc.[123]

123. Jorge Gamarra, 'Tratado de Derecho Civil Uruguayo: Responsabilidad Extracontractual. V. 7. Reparación del Perjuicio Vol. 3', Tomo XXV, *supra*, p. 175.

II. Pain and Suffering

592. Regarding this damage, it is common to separate it between physical damage and psychological damage. This division has been accepted by Uruguayan jurisprudence (when ruling, each of these sufferings are separately referred to).

593. Regarding physical pain, jurisprudence has admitted that the heirs of a victim can ask for compensation, for the time the victim suffered physical pain before dying.

594. Regarding psychological pain, heirs have also asked for compensation for victims that have been in a coma after an accident and then died (because they allege that even in a vegetative state one can also experience psychological suffering). Compensation for physical damages, normally, is very low.[124]

III. Affection Damage in Case of Death

595. This damage refers to the suffering of the closest persons to the victim at the time of the death. The law does not limit who can ask for this compensation. It has been admitted that the close family and the domestic partner have legal standing to ask for this compensation.[125]

596. The closest family can also sue for economic losses if they depended, economically, on the deceased.

IV. Affection Damage in Case of Injury

597. This damage refers to the suffering of the closest people to the victim when the victim suffers an injury but does not die. In these cases, the pain and suffering have to be exceptional to be admitted. For example, in case the victim becomes a paraplegic, in case of sexual damage that deprives his wife from having children, etc.[126]

V. Loss of Life

598. This damage refers to the damage caused to the victim for the loss of his life, the damage that would pass to his heirs.[127]

---

124. *Ibid.*, p. 243.
125. *Ibid.*, p. 263.
126. *Ibid.*, p. 323.
127. *Ibid.*, p. 241.

Chapter 5. Various Damages (Property)

599. For property damage, the law that would apply would be Article 1319 of the CC, which states that 'Every unlawful act of men that causes harm to another imposes to the individual whose wilful misconduct, fault or negligence has generated the harm, the duty to repair it.'

600. When the unlawful act has been performed with wilful misconduct, that is, with intent to harm, it constitutes a crime, when the will to harm is missing; the unlawful act constitutes a quasi-crime.

601. In one case and in the other, 'the unlawful act can be negative or positive, depending this on the duty infringed, and if it referred to a duty to do, or to refrain from doing'. Therefore, if a person suffers damage in his property (being things, animals or plants) he can ask for compensation from the tortfeasor.

Chapter 6. Interference with Collateral Benefits

602. For the damage to be repaired, it has to be real, personal and it must not have been repaired yet. But here we are not before a requirement of the damage, what is missing here is the damage itself due to the fact that, after being compensated, the damage disappears due to collateral benefits.

603. The compensation for the damage by a third party occurs, for example, when insurance is hired or when the damage is covered by the social security. When this happens, it must be decided if the duty to compensate the damage expires due to this behaviour of a third party, because it could be said that, having been compensated the damage, the offender is not obliged to repair it. But another criterion is also arguable; it has two variables: (a) to understand that the repair of the damage performed by a third party does not deprive the victim of his right to act against the offender; and (b) that the third party (and not the victim) will have the right to act against him.[128]

604. We understand that the first option is unacceptable because it contradicts a general principle according to which the victim cannot obtain a profit from the damage suffered.

§1. Insurance

605. When damage is caused and insurance covers it, it will only cover the pecuniary damage suffered. The pain and suffering and the loss of profit will normally not be compensated by the insurance.

606. Some civil authors, such as Carnelli,[129] understand that due to the fact that insurance has a compensatory nature and in the application of Article 669 of the Code of Commerce,[130] the insurer legally replaces the insured in all cases.

607. Other civil authors, such as Peirano,[131] understand that the insurance does not have a compensatory nature and, therefore, the compensatory action remains in the patrimony of the victim unless he allows the insurer to subrogate in his rights.

608. Gamarra disagrees with both positions. He understands that the Uruguayan law legally subrogates the insurer when the insurance refers to things and leaves the action in the hands of the victim when the insurance refers to people. This criterion

128. Gamarra, Tratado de Derecho Civil Uruguayo, Tomo XIX, *supra*, p. 246.
129. Carnelli, Responsabilidad del causante del daño en casos de seguro y de afiliación a sociedades de asistencia médica, DJA, 67. 46–47.
130. Article 669 of the Code of Commerce states that: 'the Insurers that have paid the loss or damage suffered to the thing insured, will subrogate the insured's in their rights to repeat from the drivers or other third parties, the damages that have suffered their things, and the insured will answer personally of every act that prejudice the rights of the insurers against those third parties.'
131. Peirano Facio, Responsabilidad Civil, *supra*, pp. 370–372.

could find its foundation in the fact that life insurance does not have a compensatory nature, considering that the sum that pays the insurer does not refer to the damage caused but consists in an abstract sum, arbitrarily fixed beforehand (which results from the capitalization of the premiums).[132]Law 19.678 of 8 November 2018, which established new rules regarding the insurance market, states in its Article 42 that the payment of the insurance to the insured, gives the insurance company the right to subrogate, but that this subrogation will not apply to the insurance referred to people, unless the tortfeasor acts with malice.

609. According to Gamarra, the compensatory nature of the insurance does not matter in order to determine the subrogation of the insurer. This responds to legislative policy, which inevitably sacrifices the insurer or the insured. The insured, according to Gamarra, has the right to collect the insurance sum and, at the same time, to sue the offender, because the amount that he receives due to this insurance is the compensation of the premiums paid by the insured. In the case of things, in Uruguay, the insurer that receives the premiums in exchange of the money that it pays to the insured will also receive a plus, which is the compensatory action against the offender.

610. But at the same time, the insured will have some advantages, because he will guard against the possibility that the offender is insolvent or cannot be identified. This way, the insured obtains a faster compensation and the subrogatory action benefiting the insurer can be taken into account for the reduction of the premiums.

611. In Uruguay, usually the zone that escapes from the legal subrogation is also included in the mechanism of subrogation, through the contract (policy), because the insurer will include a clause stating its right to subrogate the insured party in it.[133] An example of this is the Appellate Court ruling 77/2015 dated 13 May 2015, in which it is established that: 'what was not taken into account by the District Court in this case, was that a conventional subrogation was agreed upon (…) in the subrogation it is established that Ecolat Uruguay S.A. was compensated for the car accident, after the repair of the vehicle, according to the invoice identified, and has nothing else to claim against Sancor … '.

§2. Social Security

612. Uruguayan jurisprudence understands that the amount received from Social Security by the relatives of the victim, as a consequence of its death, must be reduced from the amount of the compensation. Also, it has adopted the same criterion regarding the retirement pension. This is also the opinion of the civil author Peirano Facio.[134]

132. Gamarra, Tratado de Derecho Civil Uruguayo, Tomo XIX, *supra*, pp. 247–249.
133. *Ibid.*, p. 250.
134. Peirano Facio, 'Responsabilidad Extracontractual', *supra*, p. 373.

613. Meanwhile, Professor Gamarra understands that the right to the surviving pension would rise for any cause of death and would have emerged even in the absence of this wrongdoing. In addition to this, the State serves the surviving pension (and the same can be said regarding the retirement pension) because it has an obligation to do so, in return for the amounts that the victim contributed during the time he worked.

614. Therefore, and until there is a law that establishes the right of the State to subrogate in the victim's rights, the victim should receive the pension and, in addition, maintain the right to claim for the total amount of the damage suffered. This is because the pension does not have a compensatory nature (it is paid if the death of the victim occurs due to natural causes too) and is quantified independently from the damage suffered to the heirs of the deceased.[135]

§3. Other Third Parties

I. Medical Entities

615. It has been discussed by Uruguayan jurisprudence whether an HMO can repeat against the wrongdoer the money it has expended in curing the victim of such harming act when the victim is one of its members.

616. Regarding this issue, Professor Carnelli has stated that the member of an HMO should have the possibility to file an action against the offender. Carnelli alleges that medical assistance is not a compensation because it is provided due to the contract celebrated by the victim with the HMO that obliges the victim to pay a monthly fee. Also, he affirms that the law has not established the right of the HMO to subrogate the victim, and because of this, a subrogation would not proceed.[136]

II. Liberality

617. If a person seeks to alleviate the situation of the victim with an act of generosity, the jurisprudence and civil authors agree that this person does not subrogate in the right of the victim to ask for compensation from the offender. Therefore, the victim can sue the wrongdoer for the total amount of the damages suffered (although part of them has been already compensated by the benefactor).

618. Notwithstanding this, Article 1450 of the CC states that:

> the pay can be performed not only by the debtor, but also by any interested party (…). It can also be done by a third party, not interested, that acts with

135. Gamarra, Tratado de Derecho Civil Uruguayo, Tomo XIX, *supra*, pp. 252–253.
136. Carnelli, Responsabilidad del causante del daño en casos de seguro y de afiliación a sociedades de asistencia médica, *supra*, p. 251.

the express or implied consent of the debtor. It can also be done by a third party, without the knowledge of the debtor. In this case, the third party will have the right to repeat from the debtor what was paid, but if he paid against the will of the debtor, he will not be able to repeat against him.

619. Therefore, if a third party compensates a victim as a benefactor, he will not subrogate in the victim's rights. But if the third party paid this compensation with the purpose of paying the debt of the offender, then the subrogation will proceed.

620. Regarding this issue, Professor Gamarra understands that the HMO should agree with its member on a conventional subrogation, because currently the wrongdoers are being exempted of liability due to the fact that the victim cannot claim the medical expenses incurred, because no HMO will give him the detail of the medical fees he would have paid in case he was not a member, and, on the contrary, the HMO will not sue because it does not have the right to subrogate in the victim's rights.

621. When the medical public assistance takes care of the victim, the same happens (only that in this case, the victim does not pay anything for this assistance). Gamarra considers that a law should be enacted, establishing the legal right of the HMO to subrogate the victim, and, meanwhile, a conventional subrogation should operate.[137]

137. Gamarra, 'Tratado de Derecho Civil Uruguayo', Tomo XIX, *supra*, pp. 251–252.

Chapter 7. Other Remedies

§1. Restitution for Unjust Enrichment

622. In Uruguay, a principle applies in virtue of which no one can get richer at the expense of others, and in some way, all the regulation referred to the law of obligations and contracts is inspired in this principle and seeks to impede its violation. But when a situation, which is not specifically foreseen, emerges and determines that one person gets richer (without cause) at the expense of another (the impoverished), then Article 1308 of the Civil Code allows him to file an action against the enriched party and, in this way, restore the unfairly altered balance. Therefore, this action is a residual remedy that can only be applied when there is no other remedy expressly foreseen.[138] Regarding this requirement, the Second Appellate Court, in its ruling 35/2015 dated 18 March 2015, established that: 'the claim filed by the plaintiff is of a residual remedy, and can only be filed in case a contractual or legal bond does not exist. Due to this, if the claimant understood that there was an unjust modification on the contract, he should have filed a claim for contractual liability, not for unjust enrichment'.

623. Article 1308 of the Civil Code states that any unlawful act of men that improves the condition of a person, harming another, without existing the intention of making a liberality, gives place to a quasi-contract that forces he who had improved his condition to give back the amount or thing turned into his benefit.

§2. Injunctive Relief

624. Uruguayan law establishes the right to file injunctive relief claims through two actions: the shelter action and the precautionary measure.

I. Shelter Action

625. The shelter action is regulated by Law 16.011 and states in Article 1 that:

> any person or legal entity, public or private, can file a shelter action against any act or omission of the state or semi-official authorities, as well as of individuals that currently or imminently in their opinion, harm, restrict, alter or threaten with express illegitimacy, any of his rights and liberties, acknowledged expressly or implicitly by the Constitution, except those cases in which the filing of the action of 'habeas corpus' proceeds.

626. This is also a residual action that can only be filed when there is no other remedy available to stop the threatening situation or the harm being experienced.

138. Carlos de Cores et al., 'Obligaciones y Cuasicontratos', Editorial Fundación de Cultura Universitaria, 1st ed., Montevideo, 2009, p. 318.

II. Precautionary Measures

627. Other injunctive reliefs regulated by Uruguayan laws are the precautionary measures. These measures are regulated by Article 312 of the General Procedure Code, which establishes that precautionary measures can be adopted when the court deems that they are indispensable for the protection of a right and as long as there is a risk of harm or frustration of a right due to the duration of the procedure. The existence of the right and the risk of harm must be proved summarily. Regarding the time in which these measures can be adopted, Article 311.2 of the General Procedure Code states that precautionary measures can be adopted even before the trial, but in this case, they will expire automatically if the lawsuit is not filed within thirty days from the day when they were performed. In case the precautionary measure expires, the party who asked for it will be condemned to pay the expenses of all of the procedure, and the damages caused by it.

628. Also, Uruguayan law establishes, in some specific cases, the right of the injured party to ask for precautionary measures. An example of this is Law 9.739 (Author Rights law), which establishes in Article 48, that the judge, after being asked by the owner of an author's right or his representative or legal entities of collective management, can order the performance of precautionary measures in order to prevent that an infraction is committed or to prevent the continuance of a violation already made to the exclusive rights of the owner.

§3. Punitive Damages

629. In Uruguay, the general rule is that punitive damages cannot be a part of compensation. Notwithstanding this, there is an exception to this rule.

I. Labour Proceedings

630. Article 29 of Law 18.572 establishes a fine of 10% over the amount of the credit owed in favour of the employee when the employer does not comply to pay the labour credits punctually.[139] This fine was created in order to discourage the employers from non-complying with the payment of the labour credits or from complying after the due date has passed.

139. Article 18.572 of Law 18.572: The omission of payment of the labour credits will generate automatically, from the moment in which it can be claimed, a surcharge of 10% over the amount of the credit owed.

Selected Bibliography

Achával. *Responsabilidad Civil del Médico.* 2 Edición, Buenos Aires, 1996.

Barúa, Mariana. *Legitimación Activa de Cualquier Interesado para Actuar en Representación de Intereses Difusos o Colectivos.* Uruguayan Newspaper Ultimas Noticias, 5 November 2009.

Berdaguer, Jaime, *Consultation dated 12 May 2010.* filed in a case of civil liability before the 9th Civil District Court, in the case '*Rodriguez Carril, Sylvana Sabrina and others v. Pressa, Carlos and others.* Damages' (file 2-3625/2010), p. 7.

Blengio, Juan. *La Cuestión del concurso y del cúmulo de la responsabilidad civil. Reseña sobre un tema que es conveniente volver a reflexionar.* ADCU XXVII, Editorial FCU.

Cage, Alan. *El Ciclo Económico, Breve historia económica del Uruguay.*

Carnelli, Santiago. *Reparación de los daños causados a terceros por conductores arrendatarios de vehículos de alquiler.* Anuario de Derecho Civil Uruguayo, Tomo XXXVII.

Carnelli, Santiago. *Responsabilidad del causante del daño en casos de seguro y de afiliación a sociedades de asistencia médica.* DJA, 67.

Carnelli, Santiago. *Titular activo de la responsabilidad decenal y situaciones que la misma abarca.* Anuario de Derecho Civil Uruguayo, T. XXVII.

Cordobera, Garrido. *Los Daños Colectivos y la Reparación.* Editorial Universidad, Buenos Aires, 1993.

de Cores, Carlos, Berdaguer, Jaime y otros. *Obligaciones y Cuasicontratos.* Editorial Fundación de Cultura Universitaria, 1st Edition, Montevideo, 2009, p. 318.

De Cupis, *Danno,* I, n. 13.

Diario El País webpage: *http://historico.elpais.com.uy/especiales/aniversario/1980 /1982/1.html* .

Espinoza Espinoza, Juan. *Derecho de la Responsabilidad Civil.* 2 Edición Actualizada y Aumentada, Editorial Gaceta Jurídica, Lima, 2003.

Franzoni. Degli effectti del contratto.

Gamarra, Jorge Luis and Gamarra, Jorge. *Responsabilidad Extracontractual.* Editorial Fundación de Cultura Universitaria, First Edition, Montevideo, 2007.

Gamarra, Jorge Luis, and Gamarra, Jorge. *Responsabilidad Extracontractual.* 1st. Edition, Editorial Fundación de Cultura Universitaria, Montevideo, 2007.

Gamarra, Jorge, *Tratado de Derecho Civil Uruguayo.* Tomo XXV, Editorial Fundación de Cultura Universitaria, Montevideo, 2005.

Gamarra, Jorge. *Responsabilidad del fabricante.* Anuario de Derecho Civil Uruguayo, Tomo XXVII.

Selected Bibliography

Gamarra, Jorge. *Tratado de Derecho Civil Uruguayo.* Tomo I, Editorial FCU, Montevideo, 1995.

Gamarra, Jorge. *Tratado de Derecho Civil Uruguayo.* Tomo XIX, 2 Edition, Editorial Fundación de Cultura Universitaria, Montevideo, 2012.

Gamarra, Jorge. *Tratado de Derecho Civil Uruguayo.* Tomo XX, Editorial FCU, Montevideo, 2003.

Gamarra, Jorge. *Tratado de Derecho Civil Uruguayo.* Tomo XXI, 3rd. edition, 2004, Montevideo.

Gamarra, Jorge. *Tratado de Derecho Civil Uruguayo.* Tomo XXIII, Editorial Fundación de Cultura Universitaria, Montevideo, 2007.

Gamarra, Jorge. *Tratado de Derecho Civil Uruguayo.* Tomo XXIV, Editorial Fundación de Cultura Universitaria, Montevideo, 1992.

Gamarra, Jorge. *Responsabilidad Civil Médica.* Tomo I, Editorial Fundación de Cultura Universitaria, Montevideo, 2000.

Martins, Daniel Hugo. *Constitución y Administración.* Editorial Industria Gráfica Nuevo Siglo Ltda., Montevideo, 1993.

Mello, José. *Acción directa del tercero damnificado contra el asegurador del arrendador de vehículos sin chofer.* Anuario de Derecho Civil Uruguayo, Tomo XXXIX.

Ordoqui Castilla, Gustavo. *Responsabilidad Civil del Abogado y del Escribano.* Editorial Universidad Católica del Uruguay, Montevideo, 2007.

Ordoqui Castilla, Gustavo. *Responsabilidad Civil del Profesional Liberal.* Editorial Fundación de Cultura Universitaria, 1st. Edition, Montevideo, 1993.

Peirano Facio, Jorge. *Curso de Obligaciones.* Tomo I (1957).

Peirano Facio, Jorge. *Responsabilidad Extracontractual.* (1954).

Peirano Facio, Jorge. *Responsabilidad Extracontractual.* Editorial Barreiro Ramos, Montevideo, 1954.

Peirano Facio, Jorge. *La responsabilidad civil del fabricante.* Anuario de Derecho Comercial, N 4.

Planiol. T. II, n. 863.

Prosser. *Torts.* n. 43, pp. 254–255; Fleming, An introduction.

Ramírez, Gonzalo. *La codicia y la buena fe.* published in the digital version of the Uruguayan newspaper ‘El Pais’, http://www.elpais.com.uy/economia-y-mercado/codicia-buena-fe.html.

Risso Ferrand, Martin J. *Algunas reflexiones sobre los derechos al honor, a la intimidad, a la propia imagen y la libertad de prensa.* Biblioteca Jurídica Virtual del Instituto de Investigaciones Jurídicas de la UNAM.

Sayagués Laso, Enrique. *Tratado de Derecho Administrativo.* 6th edition, Ed. Facultad de Derecho y Ciencias Sociales de la Universidad de la República y Fundación de Cultura Universitaria, Tomo I, 1988.

Sayagués Laso, Enrique. *Tratado de Derecho Administrativo.* 6th edition, Ed. Facultad de Derecho y Ciencias Sociales de la Universidad de la República y Fundación de Cultura Universitaria, Tomo I, 1988.

Uruguayan Criminal Code.

Venturini, Beatriz and others. ‘Manual de Contratos II’, article written by Beatriz Venturini and Mariana Barúa, 1st. Edition, Editorial UM Universidad de Montevideo, Montevideo, 2004.

Venturini, Beatriz and others. *Manual de Contratos II.* 1st. Edition, Editorial UM Universidad de Montevideo, Montevideo, 2004.

Venturini, Beatriz, and Szafir, Dora. *Legitimados pasivos en la responsabilidad contractual por hecho de las cosas.* Nueva lectura del art.1324 inc.1 del Código Civil, Anuario de Derecho Civil Uruguayo, Tomo XXIV.

Venturini, Beatriz. *El Daño Moral, Editorial Fundación de Cultura Universitaria.* 2nd edition, Montevideo, 1992.

Vescovi, Enrique. *Introducción al Derecho* (17th ed, 1992).

Selected Bibliography

Index

The numbers here refer to paragraph numbers.

Index

www.ingramcontent.com/pod-product-compliance
Ingram Content Group UK Ltd.
Pitfield, Milton Keynes, MK11 3LW, UK
UKHW020147290926
15471UKWH00004B/731

9 789403 5007